LEGAL PRACTICE HANDBOOK

CLIENT CARE

James Alexander, FIPM, MIMgt

Series Editor: Anthony G. King, MA, Solicitor

Director of Education, Clifford Chance

BLACKSTONE
PRESS LIMITED

First published in Great Britain 1993 by Blackstone Press Limited,
9–15 Aldine Street, London W12 8AW. Telephone 081–740 1173

© James Alexander, 1993

ISBN: 1 85431 299 5

British Library Cataloguing in Publication Data
A CIP catalogue record for this book is available from the British
Library

Typeset by Style Photosetting Ltd, Mayfield, East Sussex
Printed by BPCC Wheatons Ltd, Exeter

Contents

Preface

It has been a delightful task, writing this book. It has given me an opportunity to translate into one complete text all the practical ideas and results of research that have accumulated over several years of being quite passionate about client care.

Many client care seminars have come and gone; many swords have been crossed with reluctant participants; many enthusiastic people have gone back to work fired with a wish to improve their attention to their clients; many laughs have been shared over the idiosyncrasies of life in a law firm. Some of the book is a narrative version of seminar talk notes, other parts are actual exercises that have been productive in cementing the concepts in mind. Yet other parts have been gleaned from colleagues cleverer than I, who have unwittingly put good material my way. If any of those colleagues recognise their work here, I apologise for not acknowledging it specifically – it is probably because I have lost sight of where the original ideas came from!

My thanks are due particularly to Mick Beeby from the Bristol Business School who thrust my ideas on client care together with lawyers for the first time. Thanks also to Frank Southworth and Carol Crowdy of the Faculty of Law at the University of the West of England, Bristol; to Barbara Charnock, Carole Evans, Chris Fowler, Patricia Graham, John Hicks, Jon Holmes, Susan Holland, Tracy Newport, Stephen Roberts, Fernando Ruz, Clive Walford and many other lawyer and non-lawyer colleagues from firms large and small, law centres, Citizens Advice Bureaux and the Law Society who afforded me such a broad arena and such rich pickings for my research. It is with gratitude that I acknowledge the permission granted by Thrings and Long of Bath to use freely material from work we did together in compiling a Client Care Handbook, adapted parts of which appear anonymously here and there in the text.

Thanks are also due to new friends at Blackstone and to Tony King.

James Alexander
Dursley
February 1993

Introduction

One of the most influential business books published in the last few years is *A Passion for Excellence* by Tom Peters and Nancy Austin. Before you ever delve into the book itself, the flyleaf introduces you to a bold and provocative statement which summarises the major thrusts of the work.

Peters and Austin say that there are three secrets for organisational excellence. In order of priority – first you must have *superlative client care*, second you must be *constantly innovative* and third you must *use all the talents of your employees*. The first concern then is client care, not effective financial management, not clever systems and controls, not a world-beating product or professional service. This vital concept has been echoed in other writings that have followed Peters and Austin. The idea of concentrating effort on the people who buy your services and products is seen by many as the most influential factor in developing strong and profitable companies.

This book takes a comprehensive and purposeful look at the client care business as it applies to the law office, from the smallest sole practitioner to the larger city firms with branches in all the strategic places. Some cynicism may become apparent as the head-in-the-sand attitudes of many lawyers is mentioned but, overall, there will be a feeling of optimism, a feeling that all can be well with commitment, training and the right attitudes.

A frequent riposte when working with firms' perceptions and practices about client care has been, 'But we've been doing it for years!' or 'Client care – that's what we're all about anyway, isn't it?' My responses to such comments have necessarily been tinged with caution and I have had to disguise my sadness and anxiety for the people concerned. Owners of such beliefs are legion and are to be found in every sort of commercial enterprise, especially in those with declining fortunes and shrinking client bases!

Other people may say, 'But that is all covered by Practice Rule 15 and the Written Professional Standards on costs'. This also is a very restricted viewpoint. Both documents are vitally important and will be dealt with in the text, but client care is infinitely broader than the concepts they contain, as this book will show you.

Overall, responses from lawyers have been as varied as from any other group. Some have embraced these concepts with open arms, recognising that Peters and Austin are right, that without clients there is no work. Others have adopted the ostrich pose but generally have been persuaded eventually that they need to change their attitudes. One very elderly but sprightly retired solicitor told me with a gleam of pioneering spirit in his eyes that he wished he had attended a client care seminar years ago. It would have opened his mind to a whole new approach and 'It's not too late to start. I'll try a couple of these ideas next time I see one of my clients.' Wonderful, and proof that you never cease to learn even if you only have a few clients as old as yourself with whom to deal.

The book is intended for everyone in the law firm, solicitors, assistants, trainees, legal executives, paralegals, secretaries, receptionists, administrators, clerks and messengers, and the man who mows the lawn on Fridays. If your firm is so small that you are all of those things at once, then this book is for you too. Everyone has a deep responsibility to care for clients – it is one of the keys to corporate success.

Some sections deal with ideas and concepts that will have to be decided at the top, matters of policy, marketing and corporate image, for example. They are matters though, about which everyone in the firm will have a view and these views should be canvassed. Other aspects of client care are practices and techniques that are relevant to every member of the firm, senior or junior. Some procedures are for the receptionists and telephone operators, some for fee-earners taking instructions. It is not practicable in a book of this size to give all the answers to all the questions. You are strongly advised to pursue any particular aspects that attract you through further reading or discussion with colleagues. Try batting ideas off people you know working in other types of organisation to see how they cope with clients. Never stop learning!

There is no suggestion that this book will only be relevant to people who have just finished their law degrees and professional law courses and who are setting out to meet the public, or any other category come to that. Client care is for all, regardless of experience and seniority. It may be difficult to persuade some senior lawyers that there is anything more to learn, but they will need to keep up with their more progressive colleagues who can see the immeasurable benefits of constantly improving the quality of service and the quality of client care. The book will thus act as a source of new ideas to some and a useful revision of ideas for others – a bargain whichever way you approach it.

It is not a complicated or a long read. Some of the book is written about the things firms in general should do and some is addressed to you directly. By absorbing all the corporate and individual aspects of client care, each member of the firm will have a clearer vision of the whole programme and will be better able to play his or her part.

This is a serious book inasmuch as it seeks to promote excellent practice in law firms. However, clients are curious things and it is the odd event, the bizarre meeting, the outrageous individual that makes the business of caring for clients so varied and challenging. I have an image of a sad, dowdy, lonely solicitor slumped over a desk, gathering cobwebs for lack of clients with a 'Client Care Manual' lying discarded and scrunched up on the floor. Do not let that be you. Use this book as a guide to good practice and ensure your colleagues do too.

Chapter One

The Concept of Client Care

1.1 WHAT IS CLIENT CARE?

In a law office, client care means the carrying out of a clear policy to ensure that *all contacts between clients and members of the firm* aid the development of a positive and fruitful relationship. This book takes that basic theme as its cornerstone and develops the many facets of such policies and practices to enable every member of a law firm to play his or her part in caring for clients to the full. The ultimate objective of such a plan is substantially to increase the client base, encourage repeat business, sell further services and enhance the reputation of the firm. In money terms, client care is designed to improve the bottom line. There cannot be a legal practice in the land where that idea has no appeal, surely?

There are substantial shifts in the amount and type of work in demand in law offices. For instance, the last few years have seen reductions in property transactions but an increase in work on litigation and insolvency. The Courts and Legal Services Act 1990 and changes in the Law Society's rules on advertising have occasioned increased competition and a less restrictive approach to publicity. The need has arisen alongside these changes to take greater care of clients and to pay more attention to quality issues. This is a trend to be found also in professions and industries outside the legal profession.

There is an increasing and recognisable tendency amongst companies and enterprises of all sorts to take more care of clients and customers. The recognition of the vital importance of such people to the continuing prosperity and fortune of the business is now being seen as a matter of utmost concern. In times of economic pressures and contracting markets, the concept is even more potent.

Many organisations have posted notices around their premises proclaiming 'The Customer is King', or 'Client Care is our Future'. Detailed courses are mounted to persuade the employees of the value of client care and customer care and the necessary practices that make it happen. Policy documents are being written, staff guidance manuals are distributed, the culture of the business is being altered to encompass new beliefs. The messages seem to be getting through – witness the almost cloying 'customer care' in evidence in most hamburger establishments or in airline lounges, the increase in politeness and consideration to be found in many major retail outlets and the direct personalisation of first contact when telephoning business houses.

On the other hand, many organisations have done little more than talk about the idea and send a few people away on charm courses. Naturally, the intentions are smothered at birth and the old ways re-emerge as the norm.

Perhaps it would be sensible to discriminate between 'customer' and 'client' at this stage. The difference is minimal in terms of their need to be offered care, maybe it is simply semantic. One simplistic way of showing the distinction is to consider customers as those who buy consumer products and clients as those who buy services. A consumer product can break, fail to work or otherwise disappoint the customer and the product can usually be taken back to the vendor and some negotiation over the problem can be effected.

Clients who pay for services do not have a product as such that they can return for refund or replacement in quite the same way as purchasers of breakables.

I have defined 'client care' in a law office as contact between members of the firm and clients or potential clients that is positive, productive and which leads to better relationships. In this context, 'members' can be further defined as everyone in the firm from the equity partners to the newest clerical assistants – without exception!

'Clients' can be defined as any individuals, or any groups of people, who deal with, have dealt with or who may in the future deal with the firm.

1.2 'WE'VE BEEN DOING IT FOR YEARS!'

A frequent and blinkered response to suggestions that client care development might be needed in a particular law practice has often been, 'We don't need that, we've been doing it for years'. The fact that there are clients who call for advice is taken to equate with the idea that they *are* being cared for but this is a dangerous assumption. On a number of occasions where seminars and study days have been set up to consider client care practice, there has been strong resistance to any form of suggested improvement to the patterns already in existence. It must be said that resistance is not universal and the more enlightened members of those firms have embraced the new ideas and practices very warmly indeed.

Two schools of thought derive from the 'it's been done that way for years' syndrome:

    (a)   It is high time it was changed.

    (b)   There is a great deal of sense in maintaining well-tried and tested methods.

What is needed is a sensible mid-point approach, with the proven ways being augmented by more positive and proactive methods and practices. Change is difficult to implement. People are naturally resistant to change and many people (lawyers are no exception!) are resentful of new approaches that seem to (a) increase workload, (b) consume time, (c) erode personal style or (d) challenge long-held views and practices. None of these effects should occur when a client care programme is carefully researched, designed and implemented.

1.3 WHO SHOULD 'DO' CLIENT CARE?

Before looking in detail at policies and practices, this important point needs to be addressed. The answer is simple in the extreme – *everyone*! An early attitude survey with one law firm asked the question, 'Who do you think ought to "do" client care?'. The replies were varied and indicative of a fascinating range of beliefs:

(a) 'Well, it's the receptionists' job, isn't it!'

(b) 'Anyone the clients talk to, I suppose.'

(c) 'Certainly not me, I only work in the finance office and send out bills.'

(d) 'All the fee-earners, but some I know don't seem to have heard of it!'

(e) 'It's obvious to me that everyone in the firm should be concerned about it but maybe some of them do not know how to change their ways.'

There is *no* exception to the requirement for members of the firm to exercise the most scrupulous client care, be they equity partners, assistant solicitors, trainee solicitors, secretarial and clerical staff, post-room staff, telephonists and receptionists, messengers or any other fee, salary or wage earners!

The way the various groups of people exercise their client care practices will of course vary, but the overlaying principles remain the same. From the first tentative approaches by a member of the public to the final closing of the matter and the placing of the file in the archives, there is scope for care and concern to improve the relationship. From the opening contact from a corporate client through to the satisfactory conclusion of the matter and the final checking of the account, there is scope.

Chapter Two

The Client Expects . . .

2.1 WHAT DOES THE CLIENT EXPECT?

The first point to consider is what the client expects when (a) choosing and (b) calling on a law firm. This will be done from the point of view of both individual and corporate clients. The client's journey will be analysed to examine the expectations at different stages. The chapter will conclude with an examination of the processes of gathering information about clients in order to be clear about what policy should be adopted and how client care should be promoted and performed.

2.1.1 The individual client

In choosing a lawyer, our member of the public has a range of considerations to ponder before heading towards you:

(a)   From a *personal* standpoint, the following characteristics are probably very desirable (especially if this individual has not sought legal help before):

(i)   Help, in the person of a solicitor, is needed *now*. There should be a high degree of *availability* at times determined by the client.

The Client Expects . . .

(ii)   The legal adviser seen should be *friendly*, non-threatening, attentive and not too judgmental.

(iii)   The client needs to feel *important*, that he or she is the only concern of the solicitor when being seen and that the matter in hand is recognised as being of the utmost importance.

(iv)   There is an expectation that there will be a warm and helpful *greeting* on arrival.

(v)   The client will hope to find evidence of *trust* developing between client and solicitor.

(vi)   The client will undoubtedly be looking for a *caring* approach. Most clients have a fairly strong view of what client care is about, although these views may vary from person to person. As a caring solicitor, you should endeavour at an early stage of the relationship to find out what the client expects in terms of 'care'.

(vii)   There will certainly be a hope that a strong and effective *relationship* will develop between legal adviser and client.

(b)   From an *environmental* point of view, the client may hope for a number of factors to be present when a firm is chosen:

(i)   There may be an expectation that the premises will be comfortable, *non-threatening* and reasonably welcoming. 'Non-threatening' can be very different in its meaning to different clients and the firm will need to take account of these expectations having decided what legal niche to occupy. For instance, a person seeking help with a £500,000 claim could find a backstreet law shop very threatening, whereas furtive Fred the burglar might be loath to approach the city-centre complex of steel and glass. If each went to the other place, all might be well.

(ii)   Certainly the premises will be expected to look professional and *competent*, with adequate reception facilities clearly identifiable. People under stress need to know that they are in the right place, seeing the right people.

(iii)   Clients scarcely ever like to be open to public scrutiny like part of a peep show. There needs to be a *discreet* waiting area where the client can feel comfortable.

(iv)   Many clients look for evidence of a green or environment-ally friendly approach. If this is of interest to you or your firm, then a statement to that effect can be added to your brochures, or displayed as a notice or poster in your reception area.

(c)   There are also *financial* expectations:

(i)   As with any purchase, clients expect *value for money*. They will expect the fees to be reasonable, within their definition of the word.

(ii)   Clients will expect to have the *costs* of the service explained and presented in an understandable form.

(iii)   Clients may choose a firm on the basis of their comparative cheapness (or expensiveness, if that is the cachet), and may expect to see a tariff.

(d)   Clients will only seek legal advice when they are unable to pursue a matter on their own. Consequently they have strong expectations about the *professionalism* of the legal advisers they choose. Professionalism is an imprecise term but is generally taken to mean that the standard and quality of services provided are of a level that could be expected of professional practitioners who maintain ethical standards, objectivity and independence and whose technical ability and knowledge cannot be challenged.

(i)   Clients will expect the outcomes of their matter to be satisfactorily determined and worked for.

(ii)   There will be a hope that the best outcome will be achieved compatible with the amount of money being expended.

(iii)   Clients will expect high-quality advice, although it is often the case that they will not know what that is and therefore will have to take everything on trust.

(iv)   Clients will expect that their adviser will be committed to their cause.

Quality is another expectation from both individual and corporate clients. In *Managing the Law Firm*, Alan Pannett's companion book in this series, he states that quality is a key management issue. He identifies several reasons that have a direct bearing on client care:

(a)   Many organisations (including no doubt some of your competitors) are adopting a total quality management (TQM) approach to providing services, and are increasing their profits accordingly.

(b)   Quality emphasises the need to meet client expectations.

(c)   Quality means improved service and helps to differentiate a firm from its competitors.

(d)   Quality helps develop client loyalty.

(e)   Quality service to clients promotes efficiency and saves costs.

Note that these expectations will vary considerably from individual to individual, each according to his or her need and personal beliefs and values.

2.1.2   The corporate client

Corporate clients have many of the same expectations as individual clients, albeit to a different degree. In addition there are other expectations that the corporate client may have:

(a)   The most likely expectation is that there will be a number of points of compatibility between the client and his or her company's way of working and the law office and its way of working. ('Law office' is used here rather than 'lawyer' because the expectations will cover the whole gamut of service and attention that the clients will be seeking from reception through to the closing of the file.) The following points of compatibility are not in priority order, nor is the list exhaustive:

(i)   Technological compatibility – the sophistication of information technology and communications, the effective use of state-of-the-art business machinery and the quality and style of written material are all matters where clients will expect the legal service to match their own technological advances. The corollary of this is that a client with little technological sophistication may be overwhelmed by a slick, high-tech law office.

(ii)   Compatibility in scale – a corporate client is likely to be comforted by knowing that its company with its international connections and multifaceted operation is dealing with a law firm which operates on a similar scale. The law firm will be compared to the company's own operation to find similarities in order to avoid problems in explaining breadth (or narrowness) of interests.

(iii)   Compatibility in range of expertise – corporate clients rarely approach a law firm with a solitary problem. There will be many needs for legal advice over many types of matter, and the corporate client will need to be reassured that such a range of skills exists (but see also 2.2 for other reasons that a corporate client might choose a particular law firm).

(iv)   Compatibility of reputation – this almost speaks for itself. The high-flyers will seek to move with the high-flyers and the middle-of-the-roaders will go with the middle-of-the-roaders.

A small middle-of-the-road firm saw its market share being whittled away through lack of prestige clients. The few partners managed to persuade an up-and-coming lawyer to join them with promises of major change. Clients came too and the business burgeoned. As the reputation grew and the old shackles fell away, the pace of progress accelerated. Successful clients recognised a successful firm – they grew together.

(b)   The corporate client will also expect a high-speed response to requests for help together with almost unlimited availability and accessibility, at a reasonably high level.

(c)   Another major expectation from corporate clients is that of co-professionalism. There is a wish to deal with people who are recognised as being equally professional and highly trained and where the recognition is mutual (or is believed to be mutual!).

(d) An often overlooked but quite important issue is the expectation that there will be high standards of dress exhibited by the law office staff and partners.

One noted American writer on counselling coined the phrase 'counsellor-client cognitive congruence'. Although the phrase is unpleasantly clumsy, the concept has an element of truth about it: someone seeking help will hope to find a helper who is similar in outlook, style, gender, age and values. If the client perceives marked similarities between the two of them, there may be an acceptance, a belief, that the counsellor will be more in tune with the client's feelings and wishes than if they are noticeably different. Translated into the concepts of expectation that we have just been examining, there is a need for law firms seriously to examine their images and styles to ensure that their targeted clients actually see what they expect, rather than seeing something that might repel instead of attract.

2.2 WHY CHOOSE THIS FIRM?

Law firms choose whether to be generalist or specialist with a view to attracting a particular group of clients (see also chapter 4 on marketing). However attractive for whatever reason, the choice still rests with the client. However much the idea might be resisted or pooh-poohed by older members of the firm, the market for legal advice is becoming far more competitive and firms that do not recognise the value of client care and correct marketing will go to the wall.

An individual client will choose a law firm when most of the expectations listed above would seem to be likely to be met, after checking out several firms. Where it is not cruical to obtain a lawyer within the hour, the same principles will apply to lawyer choosing as to buying major consumer durables – research and enquiry (window shopping or catalogue browsing), comparisons, choice, action (purchase). An understanding of these processes can assist the law firm in setting itself within the market and in deciding its marketing strategy.

Ignoring the processes of purchase can be disastrous as *there will be no clients!*

The processes of purchase may be different for corporate clients. Alan Pannett identifies 'passive' and 'active' reasons for business clients choosing a particular firm. Passive reasons include:

(a)   Inertia – 'We have always used that firm' (a possible source of delight for the firm struggling to survive!).

(b)   Parent company choice imposed on subsidiary company (any form of imposition makes for less sound relationships, often starting off on the wrong foot, as with arranged marriages, imprisonment or compulsory purchase).

(c)   Acquired companies keeping their usual firm.

(d)   Choice of the largest firm, for safety (but with potential for incompatibility).

(e)   Choice of the local firm.

Active reasons include:

(a)   Selection according to the reputation of the firm and/or individual partners.

(b)   Seeking recommendations through personal contacts and advisers such as accountants.

(c)   Checking out a firm's reputation by talking with their clients.

(d)   Contacting firms who send out 'beauty contest' brochures or following a tendering service presentation.

These activities are totally compatible with best purchasing practice – business clients are as canny with their money over buying legal advice as they will be over purchasing raw materials.

Pannett also identifies factors that will influence a move from passive to active choice:

(a)   The arrival of new problems where specialist help is needed, such as with EC or environmental law.

(b)   Where there is greater mobility of partners in law firms through mergers and moves.

(c)   Where there is *stronger marketing* by law firms.

(d)   When *quality and client care* have assumed considerable and recognisable importance.

These factors can equally lead a business to change its legal advisers. Change may also be occasioned by:

(a)   Deterioration in the relationship or a change of personnel.

(b)   A failure of the firm to anticipate the client's needs – a classic example of bad client care.

(c)   The client's need for a larger firm to match its growth.

(d)   Inefficiency, poor quality control or any aspect of the relationship that makes for client dissatisfaction, such as delays, missed opportunities or poor communication.

2.3   THE CLIENT'S JOURNEY

To assist with filling in the backcloth against which the many facets of client care are acted out, it is necessary to follow a client from the point when a decision has been made to choose a particular firm, and see what happens up to the point when the matter is finished. This journey will highlight a range of activities that the firm must consider when making client care a principal concern and a part of good practice.

The stages of the journey are:

(a)   Arrival at the firm – this can be in person at the reception area or by telephone in the first instance. The initial interaction between firm and client has a major influence on the way the relationship will develop and the way the client perceives the correctness or otherwise of the initial choice. This involves reception and telephone skills.

(b)   First meeting – whether with a solicitor immediately or with another person, the first introduction of the matter to be discussed is often difficult for the client and the adviser. This involves interviewing and questioning skills.

(c)   Subsequent meetings – maintaining the relationship as the matter progresses is vital to ensure that the client is content with the work being done.

(d)   Closing interviews – the wrapping up of all loose ends and the efficient conclusion of the matter, with acceptable billing and final letters, are important for ensuring client satisfaction and loyalty.

All these skills and techniques are covered in this book, mostly in chapter 5.

It is worth pointing out that most clients will avoid going to see a lawyer if at all possible! You therefore have a strong duty to make the client comfortable at every stage of his or her journey and to help the client believe that going to the lawyer will produce positive benefits. From the start of the relationship, you must make every effort to understand the client's issues and problems and explain your issues and problems clearly to the client.

2.4   WHO ARE THE CLIENTS?

Before considering the formulation of a client care policy and codes of practice for a firm, it is essential for the firm to make a careful analysis of its client base. This needs to be done from two angles: first, there must be an analysis of known facts (and where the needed facts are not known, then research must be done); second, there should be information gathered about the service given, but from the clients' viewpoint. A comprehensive approach to client satisfaction surveys is outlined in 7.2. These can be used just as effectively before policy is made as for a post-operation review. The principles and techniques are the same for both.

2.4.1 What is already known within the firm?

Traditional reticence about prying into the affairs of other people has been hard to overcome, even amongst lawyers. Generally the only information gleaned from clients has been in direct reference to the matter in hand, and this usually has been the task of the fee-earner handling the case. Information about the clients as individuals, their needs for legal advice and their expectations of the firm and the possible outcomes were rarely known in the past.

Nowadays, however, the crucial importance of client care is recognised and the quality of the service offered is vital to the firm's success and very survival in an increasingly competitive market. Knowledge of the firm's clients is essential to the success of a client care strategy. This information can be gathered under a number of heads and, with the present sophistication of even relatively simple business computers and their associated programs, the tasks of creating such a database and conducting relevant analyses are well within the reach of every firm.

The assembly of the database should be assigned to one individual in the first instance, to ensure consistency of style and a high level of commitment. It can be a fairly onerous task, but once completed, the database can be updated easily and maintained as an essential management tool.

The analysis is just as important for individual clients as for business clients. It would not be practical to analyse data on every single client, so the analyst will need to exercise discretion in choosing subjects for the investigation. The survey can be very useful if also done according to the matter(s) being dealt with – this will assist in pinpointing particular sectors of the market and identifying specific niches for development. These areas (fields) can be identified by the computer and reported upon separately.

The following details can be gathered:

(a) What is the nature of the client's business? This is equally valuable information for individual and corporate clients. It will assist in deciding which industrial and commercial sectors to penetrate, where specific knowledge and skills can be focused or where they are lacking.

(b) On what matter(s) has the firm advised the client? This information can be quite detailed, especially in relation to business clients, to give evidence of the breadth of service and the effectiveness of cross-selling, for instance. Did dealing with the matter demand specialist experience or expertise?

(c) Why was the firm chosen in the first place? This set of responses can be vital in evaluating marketing and advertising strategies as well as giving clues about reputation and public awareness.

(d) How was contact first made? This information provides useful feedback on patterns of response and communication.

(e) Who are the major participants in the relationship, from the firm and the client company? Are there specific facts that would assist in providing better client care?

(f) Does the client use other law firms? If so, which ones and why? How different is their business from ours?

(g) What known opportunities exist for expanding the work done for this client, in terms of more of the same or in a different area? What opportunities are suspected as potential areas for expansion?

(h) For clients that are not currently active, when was the last contact? Is renewed contact desirable? When?

Chapter Three

Promoting a Client Care Policy

3.1 A WRITTEN POLICY STATEMENT

For any client care programme to be effective, the firm must have a clearly stated policy, outlining the essential features and philosophy behind the need for and provision of client care. This policy document should be in the form of a simply worded and readily available statement that encapsulates the firm's intent and practice.

A popular concept in organisational practice is the 'mission statement' – a statement which embodies the primary aims of the organisation and stands alone as the principal guiding light for all that the members in the organisation do and think. In spite of some reluctance amongst partners to consider such a thing, there are great advantages in setting down the long-term aim and purpose of the firm together with specific objectives to help achieve them. It would be quite acceptable to produce a 'client care policy' in such a format, as an integral part of the mission statement. This would enable all the lawyers and non-lawyers in the firm to recognise the importance attached to client care and relate their jobs and specific responsibilities in this area to a global or organisation-wide approach. The policy statement will act as a focus for actions and a spur to improve communications; it will remove ambiguities and uncertainties and outline specific areas of activity.

The following is an example of such a global client care policy statement:

This firm aims to be the principal provider of legal services to the public in this area and we commit ourselves to offering the very best of care to all clients, from the private individual to corporate clients from industry and commerce.

To do this, we intend to provide a quality service, of utmost integrity and responsiveness, upholding traditional standards of thoroughness and enterprise. We recognise the vital importance of our clients to our success as legal advisers. We equally recognise the vital importance of ourselves and our services to our clients' well-being and satisfaction. Every effort will be directed by all members of the firm to achieve these aims.

3.1.1 Designing the policy statement

A client care policy statement needs to be thought through and written most carefully to encapsulate the intentions of the firm and to provide a clear remit to the partners and staff. Clearly, one firm's ideal will not be another's – objectives and practices will vary. Within one firm, beliefs about client care as well as practices may vary from department to department and indeed from solicitor to solicitor! It is only by having a carefully prepared and universally distributed policy and code of practice that levels of performance can be standardised throughout the firm.

The wording of a client care policy statement should be clear and unambiguous. It should be meaningful to every member of the firm, no matter what job is held. It is the firm's encompassing client care statement from which all activities and practices will spring. Writing such a document presupposes an amount of research and policy consideration, so it should not be a hurried exercise. It may follow the writing of a mission statement and form a part of it. However, the absence of a mission statement should not prevent a client care policy being written.

3.1.2 A client care policy group

In order to produce an acceptable and realistic response, there should be a client care policy group set up to look at all matters of client care and to promote the very best practice in this area. To achieve a rounded view, representative of all shades of opinion, such a group might consist of:

(a) A senior partner.
(b) The partner with overall responsibility for training.
(c) A more junior fee-earner.
(d) A secretary or member of the support staff.
(e) A receptionist.

Experience has shown that such a multi-level group has enough experience and interest to consider and evaluate all aspects of client care, with input from several differing points of view. It is not too large to be clumsy and, with luck, times should be found when all are available to meet.

The group needs a broad remit to be effective, with a clear line of reporting to the managing partner. Its first task will be to design the policy statement.

Schemes effecting organisational change, whether of a structural, philosophical, practical or directional nature, seem to do better with a champion. Such a person is one who is single-mindedly obsessed with the concept, is a tireless worker towards its achievement and who can inspire and motivate others to espouse the same cause. Champions are not appointed, they announce themselves at every opportunity (occasionally to the exasperation of colleagues!). They tend also to be creative types, vocal and persuasive, with good contacts inside and outside the organisation. If you can find your champion of client care in your firm then you need to add a sixth line to the membership of the client care group:

(f) The champion.

It may indeed be appropriate to make the champion the coordinator of the group, even if he or she is not the most senior person in the team. This is a favourite concept within project management – the leader being the champion or the person with the greatest commitment to the project's success.

Some resources should be made available to the policy group in order to produce a worthwhile policy statement and, as we will examine later, a code of practice.

3.1.2   Publishing the policy statement

Once the text of a client care policy statement is agreed, it should be produced in the form of an internal memorandum addressed individually to all staff (this really means *all* staff!), with a note that training and other activities to promote the concepts and practices of client care are to follow. It is no good producing a policy statement as if it was the only thing needed, to be able to say, 'Of course we have client care! We have a policy!'

There is a strong case also for promulgating the client care policy statement to a wider population than just members of the firm. For example, it could be sent to:

(a)   Existing active clients – by an insert with current correspondence (sadly, some clients may have to be excluded – especially if progress in their matter so far is not all that they would wish!).

(b)   Existing but non-active clients – this could be a useful reminder to past clients that you still exist and are still offering an excellent and above-average service. The policy statement could be incorporated into a general, keeping-in-touch reminder letter (see also 4.3 on marketing).

(c)   Potential clients – an artworked, framed notice could be displayed effectively in the reception area, or strategically in corridors, entrances or external street-level windows.

(d)   The public at large – by press releases or advertising material. The promotion of a sound and effective client care policy could well be the basis of an excellent piece of editorial copy for local papers or business magazines, helping to give your firm that extra edge in a competitive environment. Frequently, editors will offer space for copy if the writers also pay for a small advertisement. Look out for special features on legal services or services to businesses. Ask for details of forthcoming special editions or focus pages.

In chapter 2, the client's journey was examined, with emphasis on the reasons for the client's choice of lawyer. A positive and encouraging client care policy, prominently published, will draw in new clients and persuade ex-clients to return for further advice.

3.2 DEVELOPING THE POLICY INTO PRACTICE

There are many practical implications when elaborating the simple policy statement into a workable and effective set of specific practices. This will largely be the remit for the client care group, with others brought in to help as appropriate. When it comes to specific areas of activity the partner with oversight of that function will need to be consulted. So also will people actively pursuing the practices at present. Activities will include:

(a) Analysing the firm's present practices and procedures for client care. This can be done effectively with a staff survey (see 4.2.1 for a helpful set of questions), or through departmental or sectional meetings or working parties set up for the purpose. Everyone should be given the opportunity to contribute ideas and preferences.

(b) Devising improved systems and procedures. Frequently the survey or meetings will throw up bad practices and inadequate attention to client care. The client care group needs to address these matters urgently and, in consultation with the appropriate people, revise practices and procedures.

(c) Writing a staff client care handbook. This should contain a wealth of practical advice to all members of the firm and serve as a reference source to standardise practice (see 3.2.1).

(d) Devising and installing a programme of training for all members of the firm (see 3.3).

The same team that devised the policy should be instrumental in organising these activities and producing the client care handbook for the firm.

Research with law firms of all sizes and complexities shows that there is no one in any firm who does not have a responsibility to foster good

ctice and perform all duties and functions with the
. The client's journey examined in chapter 2 showed
how   ould be made at every level and with every department
in the firm, from initial telephone calls to finally receiving a bill.

Because everybody in the firm is involved, the firm's client care
handbook must be broad enough to encompass everyone's responsibilities and yet detailed enough to make the client care practices
realistic and effective.

3.2.1 Outlines of a client care handbook

There is no one perfect way that a client care handbook should be
compiled, but the following list of contents would produce a sound,
comprehensive and usable book, of value to all members of the firm.

(a) A general statement of the firm's policy about client care, with
a personal statement of commitment from the senior or managing
partner.

(b) A brief introduction to the firm and its history, emphasising
its background and reputation, the major areas of activity and the
part played in the local community, for example.

(c) The ongoing need to acquire new business and ways of
encouraging new and existing clients to seek services.

(d) Dealing with new clients – from first contacts to first
interviews – the parts played by all in the firm.

(e) Communicating with clients – the specific ways of interacting
with clients to their and your best advantage and effect.

(f) Communicating with colleagues – maintaining good internal
relations and developing mutual understanding and concern.

(g) The professional skills involved in working with clients.

(h) Closing files and follow-up procedures.

(i)   Costs and billing clients.

(j)   Managing and organising yourself.

(k)   Evaluation of client care procedures and practices.

In all probability, the major parts of your handbook will be sections (d), (e), (f) and (g) and great care needs to be taken to ensure that the right concepts and practices are outlined and explained. Research will be needed in the firm to establish exactly what is done – or what should be done! – before committing procedures to paper.

Most of these ideas and practices are described in detail elsewhere in this book, affording a useful source upon which to draw when writing your handbook.

Many firms are intending to apply for accreditation to BS5750 with the British Standards Institute to demonstrate the quality of management and operations. This is a standard that is likely to be sought more and more by corporate and overseas clients in their law firms. The Law Society has produced *Quality: a Briefing for Solicitors*, a set of guidelines for firms wishing to seek this accreditation. Included in the list of requirements are (a) a 'quality manual' documenting the firm's systems in every detail and (b) training in client care. The proposals in this book will go a long way towards meeting those requirements.

3.2.2   Publishing the handbook

The style and presentation of the handbook are very much matters of individual taste. However, it should be produced in a form that suggests that the whole business of client care is regarded very seriously and is given great emphasis within the firm. This does not preclude the introduction of some appropriate humour or illustrations to make a point – some of the best client care manuals have been well illustrated and the effect is to emphasise the techniques rather than detract from them.

Many people in organisations, law firms included, display an unwarranted scepticism about the value of client care policies and procedures. Yet their very livelihoods depend on a regular supply of fresh clients and customers, without which the future would look very bleak indeed.

The managing partner must give the handbook his or her imprimatur and ideally add an injunction at the front that it is the duty of all members of the organisation to exercise the greatest effort towards the client care policy and practices outlined within. Without complete commitment from the very top, the exercise will lose momentum and eventually collapse.

The physical form of the handbook needs to be such that members of the firm will keep it by them at their desks and refer to it regularly. In-house photocopying may suffice, provided that it is of very high quality, and an A4 format is recommended. The booklet should be given a neat and recognisable title page and bound within a good cover either by comb-binding or by heat-sealing.

If a formalised programme of client care is new to your firm, it could well be to everyone's advantage to launch the new handbook at a special event. Possible options for this would be:

(a)   The first in a series of training seminars on client care.

(b)   A meeting after work when most people could be present for half an hour.

(c)   A series of smaller departmental meetings held over a short period of time.

Whatever you decide to do, emphasise the great advantages to your clients of the improved levels of care, which in turn enhance everyone's future by ensuring an increase in the client base and the continuance of the firm.

3.3   TRAINING FOR IMPROVED CLIENT CARE

Even if there is a reasonably high level of awareness of client care and all the associated practices, the introduction of a new client care handbook is an excellent opportunity to mount some effective in-house training for all members of the firm.

3.3.1 Who should present it?

There are several options for the role of trainer:

(a)   The most obvious is the firm's training or education partner, the director of education or training, or education manager, although many smaller practices do not have such a person.

(b)   An existing member of the firm – but there must be one proviso, that the person chosen is competent at training and running sessions where maximum benefit can be obtained. Many organisations use senior staff (because they are senior staff!) to run courses, with disastrous results. 'Experts' are not necessarily first-class trainers. People from within who might be appropriate (if they can train) are:

(i)   The champion, whose enthusiasm will be infectious.

(ii)   The partner with responsibility for training.

(iii)   The senior partner.

(c)   Someone from outside the firm – a recognised consultant trainer who has a keen working knowledge of client care practices and ideally also with a sound working knowledge of legal firms and lawyers.

The legal practice course (LPC) from September 1993 onwards and the professional skills course (PSC) from July 1994 will both contain elements of client care either explicitly or implicitly. The LPC must include a minimum of 25 per cent of skills training on the grounds that a trainee solicitor must receive training not only in substantive law and procedures but also in the skills necessary to carry out such tasks. The course identifies five areas – practical legal research, writing and drafting, interviewing, advocacy and negotiation – which will be assessed. The PSC course forms part of the training contract between the trainee solicitor and the firm and includes modules on personal work management, advocacy and oral communication skills, and professional conduct.

3.3.2   Who should attend it?

The answer to this question is simple – everyone! Experience in several organisations where the client care training programme has been mandatory, has shown this to be most powerful in getting the essential message across. The trainer may be faced with a few reluctant or sceptical course members, but generally they will be outnumbered and outvoted.

There are several ways of arranging delegation to training sessions, dependent upon the size of the firm:

(a)   All members of the firm attend a special meeting together. (A successful plan has been to run sessions from 4.00 p.m. to 7.00 p.m., thus asking for a little of the individuals' private time as well as giving a chunk of working time to the event.)

(b)   Training sessions run for departments or sections.

(c)   Sessions run for differing levels of seniority – but never omit the most senior level! They are the people who add weight to the client care programme and whose commitment will act as a spur to the rest of the firm. 'Do' them first!

(d)   The most favoured pattern for training in client care (remember the composition of the client care group) is the 'diagonal slice'. This involves setting up sessions for very mixed groups from different departments and at different hierarchic levels. The resultant range of interests and experiences will enrich the sessions and provide greater insight into the problems and practices at various points in the firm. The ideal size for the group is about a dozen. This number gives everyone a chance to speak and does not create too much of an inhibiting factor, even if senior partners are present. (Some diagonal slice seminars have proved to be the first occasion when senior partners had ever spoken to some of the more junior members of their firms! This has got to be a good thing!)

3.3.3   Where should it be held?

Ideally, all company training should be held off the firm's premises to ensure a complete absence of interruptions and an opportunity to complete the work without people slipping off 'to see a client'! However, this is rarely possible, so the board room or a comfortable spare office may be used. The trainer must ensure that everyone can be easily accommodated and that there are the necessary resources such as flip-boards, paper and pens and refreshments if needed. With much material to cover in a short time, it is essential that the resources are well organised in advance, to avoid time-wasting and loss of motivation.

3.3.4   What should it cover?

For an in-house client care training programme, the following elements should be covered:

(a)   A reiteration of the firm's client care policy statement and the way client care fits into the overall organisational philosophy, mission and business plan.

(b)   An explanation of the crucial importance of client care in this competitive and market-oriented world.

(c)   The importance of every member of the firm playing the fullest part towards a programme of client care – pointing out that each person can develop more fully professionally by taking greater care of clients.

(d)   The range of interactions between client and firm, from the first tentative call to the final settlement of the account – how each person can develop personal skills to exhibit greater client care. This will be the greatest part of the session, occasioning a deal of discussion and debate. Use must be made of the variety of experiences and roles to increase mutual understanding and recognition of mutual dependence and trust.

(e)   Proposals and suggestions for improving client care.

(f)   Dealing with complaints and difficult clients.

(g)   Evaluating the client care programme.

In the light of the constant pressures of work and the complexities of running a successful law firm, it may be optimistic to expect that a full day could be put to this exercise. However, structuring an effective and creative programme of client care can bring about such an enormous long-term gain, that merely offering the odd hour to training would be short-sighted in the extreme and very damaging to the bottom line.

3.4   FOLLOW-UP TO TRAINING

Having launched a client care programme, it is vital to continue to put pressure upon everyone to carry it out. The sceptics will be looking for gaps between what was promised and what is apparently being done. The client care group has an ongoing role to play in monitoring the programme and the senior partner must be vigilant in encouraging all to work at it. When it has become an integral part of the firm's culture, then the programme can be judged a success, but not before! Care must also be taken to ensure that client care training is built in as part of every newcomer's induction training.

The processes of evaluating the client care programme of improved responsibilities and practices are covered fully in chapter 7.

Chapter Four

The Firm

4.1 PATTERNS OF ORGANISATION

The final clutch of analyses which are needed before considering the complexities and techniques of delivering client care are to do with the organisation of the firm itself. Before you can decide how to install new or improved patterns of working in the firm you need to know a great deal about its structure, standards, style, image and value systems. This chapter will look at all of these elements in order to develop a comprehensive overview of the whole firm, its component parts and the personnel involved.

The quality of client care depends on the commitment given to it by every member of the firm from junior clerks to equity partners. This commitment is dependent upon several organisational factors:

(a) Traditional versus client-oriented organisation.

(b) Authoritative versus participative management style.

(c) Scale and departmentalisation.

(d) Personal organisation and time management.

(e) Prioritising.

(f) Delegation and teamwork.

These will be examined in turn.

4.1.1 Traditional or client-oriented?

Many organisations have not yet grasped the crucial fact that success depends almost entirely on those people who buy the goods or services that the organisation provides, and on their continuing to do so. The traditional, if-they-don't-want-to-come-they-needn't stance is fatal.

Recall Tom Peters's recipe for long-term excellence – superior client service, constant innovation and full use of the abilities of every employee, and in that order!

When comparing a traditional, head-in-the-sand organisation that does not espouse these principles, and one oriented towards positive client care, for instance, several factors emerge as having different emphases in the two types of structure. On figure 4.1 you can mark your organisation on a scale of five points from 'traditional' to 'client-oriented' on each of these factors. Totalling the scores will give a percentage effectiveness in 'client-oriented-ness'.

Figure 4.1   Traditional or client-oriented?

TRADITIONAL STRUCTURE	CLIENT-ORIENTED STRUCTURE
Decisions are generally dropped from on high, with little lower responsibility for variation or initiative.	Decisions are made at appropriate levels, based on the overall strategic vision of the firm.

1   2   3   4   5

Information tends to flow downwards only, with resultant puzzlement and some resentment.	There is a very free and full flow of information in all directions, allowing everyone to be completely *au fait* with policies, trends and feelings.

1   2   3   4   5

TRADITIONAL STRUCTURE	CLIENT-ORIENTED STRUCTURE
Management roles are seen mainly as directive and controlling.	Management is seen as a device for enabling fee-earners and staff to interact effectively with each other, as well as with clients.

$$1 \qquad 2 \qquad 3 \qquad 4 \qquad 5$$

Organisation structures are tall, in the sense that there are many hierarchic levels from top to bottom. There is empire building and much rivalry and competition.	The organisation structure is fairly flat – there are few hierarchic levels. There are no empires.

$$1 \qquad 2 \qquad 3 \qquad 4 \qquad 5$$

Training may be an issue, but only for more junior people. It is more likely a case of 'they do not need it'.	Training is certainly a vital issue for teams, individual fee-earners and staff at all levels, whether clocking up hours or not.

$$1 \qquad 2 \qquad 3 \qquad 4 \qquad 5$$

Members of the firm are kept very much in the dark as to corporate objectives.	All members of the firm are made well aware of corporate objectives and decisions, and the parts they can play towards achieving them.

$$1 \qquad 2 \qquad 3 \qquad 4 \qquad 5$$

There is no liaison between people in direct contact with clients to assess reactions, approaches and successes.	Fee-earners meet regularly to consider strategies and accountabilities for client contact. Other staff are regularly brought in as appropriate.

$$1 \qquad 2 \qquad 3 \qquad 4 \qquad 5$$

TRADITIONAL STRUCTURE	CLIENT-ORIENTED STRUCTURE

There is little or no investment in resources to encourage and develop client contact skills for those people in need of them.

Considerable resources and effort are directed to developing client care policies and practices, through injections of cash and training.

1   2   3   4   5

Recruitment policies do not account for the need for experience, personal qualities and training for those in direct contact with clients.

People are selected for their technical and professional skills as well as their interpersonal skills (including all those in front-line* positions)

1   2   3   4   5

Courtesy is scarce; clients are not listened to; clients are seen as numbers or cyphers; costs are all; clients do not come back.

Every visitor or client is shown every courtesy; they are listened to attentively; needs are met; they are people; they do come back.

1   2   3   4   5

*'Front-line' is a phrase used in industry and commerce to mean the people in direct contact with customers and clients. In a law office it can mean anyone who interacts with clients, be they receptionists, secretarial staff, clerks or fee-earners.

If you have scored 5 at every scale, you are either working for the absolutely perfect firm or you are being over-optimistic and blinkered in the extreme! It would be fair to say though, that the firm which managed a high total score was well along the road towards excellence in client care. This type of analysis can be used several ways:

(a)   By marking your perception of where your firm actually appears along each scale between the traditional view and the more enlightened one, you can produce a profile of the organisation.

(b)   By marking a point on each scale where you would like to see your firm, you can produce a projected, wished-for profile. Note that this does not necessarily have to be at the extreme 'good' end of the scale every time – this might be quite unachievable!

(c)   Where your actual profile coincides well with your projected one, there is little need for attention, other than in keeping up the desired levels of performance. Where there is a divergence between the two marks, there is cause for concern. The greater the gap, the greater the need for remedial action.

(d)   The list of factors (the client-oriented ones, that is) can be used as a checklist of effectiveness in organisational patterns that militate for better client care. They do represent good practice.

4.1.2   Authoritative or participative management?

There is a strong correlation between the quality of 'colleague care' and the quality of client care to be found in an organisation. Where there are good internal relationships, high levels of trust, interdependence or independence as needed, a strong sense of belonging and a common commitment to success, there is likely also to be good practice of client care. The quality of internal care can be assessed under several heads:

(a)   Is confidence shown in subordinates? Do people feel free to talk to senior partners? Are less senior people's ideas sought and used? Are the skills and knowledge of all partners and staff fully utilised? (What are the patterns of *leadership*?)

(b)   Does cooperative teamwork exist? Is responsibility for achieving the firm's goals felt and exercised at all levels? Is there evidence of the use of threats, fear or punishment? Are rewards encouraging? Is morale good? Are people involved? (What are the patterns of *motivation*?)

(c)   Are people informed adequately of policies, philosophies and changes? How well is downward communication received? Do people talk to one another about successes as well as problems? Are there sources of help and support when needed? How aware are the partners of the problems faced by the support staff? (What are the patterns of *communication*?)

(d)   Is decision-making a shared responsibility at the appropriate levels? Are all people in the firm asked about change and invited to participate in solving problems? (What are the patterns of *decision-making*?)

(e)   Are all fee-earners and staff involved in goal-setting? Is there any covert resistance to corporate goals? Do people appraise one another and share in each other's goal-setting? Are all newcomers fully apprised of the firm's goals and mission? (What are the patterns of *goal-setting*?)

(f)   Are review and control shared responsibilities or do they come from above? Are there informal organisations resisting the formal one? Are control data used for policing and monitoring or for assisting decisions and for self-guidance? (What are the patterns of *control*?)

A thorough review of your firm against these six sets of questions will reveal the extent of mutual trust and concern to be found within.

(a)   Where the answers elicited lead you to a gloomy and distressing view of the firm, the overall style is likely to be *authoritarian* and *exploitative* with a wide psychological gap between the partners and the staff.

(b)   Where the answers are generally positive, then the style of the organisation is likely to be more *consultative* or even fully *participative*. Undoubtedly, the latter finding will be indicative of the high probability of the firm also being good at client care. The two tend to go hand-in-hand.

Each law firm has its own feel, its own mores and cultural expectations and beliefs. These are most acutely noticed by newcomers when they accidentally break conventions and tread on established toes. Ask yourself how you would describe the climate in the firm. Is it best defined as warm, encouraging, supportive, sunny, embracing, cosy or as frosty, tense, stormy, stressful, unsympathetic, cliquish, collusive, incestuous, unhealthy?

The first list will encourage similar approaches to clients – but so will the second list! (See also 5.7 on climate and 5.10 on colleague care.)

4.1.3 Scale, departmentalisation and geography

Client care is not just for the big boys! The independent solicitor with one or two assistants will need to pursue the same policies and practices as the multinational partnership with coverage of every conceivable field of legal advice. The relationship between a sole solicitor and his or her client may be deeper because a range of different matters will all have to be dealt with by the one person. In a larger firm this is less likely with different tasks being assigned to different departments.

The larger organisations will probably be able to allocate more time and money to training for client care than smaller firms and the range of support materials can be wider and more available. Small firms could usefully combine and produce training and publicity materials on a consortium basis. There are many university law departments and independent consultants who would willingly assist a group of smaller law firms to produce very effective training in client care.

With firms that have a dispersed workforce or a heavily compartmentalised structure, there will be a need for careful harmonisation of the client care programme. This will be the task of the project coordinator mentioned in 3.1.2. There is a danger that some parts of the organisation will move at a different pace from others with resultant confusions not only for the partners and staff but also for the clients. They may receive differing treatment from departments which will not encourage loyalty and commitment.

A further problem for larger firms is the range of approaches that might be adopted by the senior partners managing different departments. The not-so-funny line about the head of litigation hating the sight of the head of property is still applicable here and there. These two can create different cultures in the two departments, with seriously differing views about matters like client care and even colleague care. The coordinator may have to use the utmost diplomacy in dealing with the two hoary old patriarchs!

The following areas of organisational and personal analysis are adequately dealt with elsewhere in the Legal Practice Handbook series (companions to this volume) but merit a summary here with particular reference to client care.

4.1.4 Personal organisation and time management

Every fee-earner and member of staff owes it to him or herself to be orderly in conducting the day's business. Much time is wasted by failures to plan work, arrange meetings correctly, use diaries effectively, inform colleagues of absences and other important facts, control interviews or leave time for writing and reading. There are excellent books and courses on time management. Such is the nature of a solicitor's work, that mismanagement of self can only lead to the client being hurried or dealt with cursorily, with instructions being very poorly taken and vital clues being missed. A solicitor who has problems in mind other than the matter in hand will lose clients.

4.1.5 Prioritising

Prioritising is a difficult task but one which is vital for presenting a professional approach. You owe it to your clients to be available when needed (compatible with all your other duties) and doing things in the right order can greatly help your personal management.

Methods such as the four-D system (do, delay, delegate or dump) may be oversimplifying an important process, but you must be able to say which of the current tasks has priority. One effective way is to grade tasks according to two dimensions, urgency and importance. A simple grid like the one in figure 4.2 helps with the process.

Tasks need to be evaluated according to the two dimensions and allocated to whichever box (category) is appropriate. This can be a start-of-day task which will set you up well for the rest of the day. Remember that it is preferable to handle a piece of paper only once – deal with it there and then.

	Very important	Fairly important	Not important
Very urgent	A	C	E
Fairly urgent	B	D	G
Not urgent	F	H	I

Figure 4.2   Prioritising grid

The allocations can now be seen as giving you the clear order of work. Do any **A** tasks first, then **B** and **C** tasks and so on in alphabetical order through to the **I** tasks at the very end. This guarantees that urgency and importance are balanced. Inevitably there will be tasks arriving through the day that were not known about at the commencement. These must be prioritised as were the original tasks and slotted into the schedule appropriately. All tasks from **A** to **F** have a high degree of urgency or importance, so should be done within the day if at all possible. Other tasks often become relegated to the next day (week?) and need to be reassessed then or abandoned altogether.

A simpler way of prioritising is to do work passed on by the most senior person first and then the work from the noisiest delegator or the one who can cause you most trouble!

4.1.6   Teamwork and delegation

Although the majority of solicitors pursue their client work individually, there is nevertheless a constant need for the support of a team of colleagues, be they fellow fee-earners or secretarial or administrative staff. None can do without the other and it is presumptuous of any of them to assume that they can. Lawyers often assume attitudes which suggest a superior intelligence or an indispensable role. This is arrogant and should be recognised as unrealistic and demotivating.

The success of the firm, particularly when measured in terms of the care extended to clients, is completely dependent on the effective cooperation of all concerned with a particular client or matter. You may not see your immediate working group as a team in the sporting sense of the word, but there are strong similarities. Each will have a specific role to play and an exclusive area of knowledge and skill; each will need the support and encouragement of the rest; each is dependent on the others for proper and effective communications. The striker will not score goals without the right passes and the right moves from the mid-fielders.

When delegating work, remember to tell the recipient of that work what is expected and by when. Do not delegate to someone who does not have the knowledge or the resources to complete the work. Remember also to tell the client if new colleagues are brought in to work on the matter or if delays are likely because you have allocated the work elsewhere.

4.2 IMAGE

Image is vitally important in establishing patterns of client care – the image of the firm as seen from within and without. In many cases the image of the firm has been developed over years of growth and merger, expansion and modernisation. Often the image was created by the founding partner and has been elaborated by successors. It may be dynamic and progressive, stolid and middle-of-the-road or fusty and cobwebbed.

As with any product or service, the purchasers, be they clients or customers, will only be attracted to that product or service if it appeals at the time the purchase is needed. It is quite possible to admire a product from afar and recognise that the vendor has quality and service on his side, but if you do not need that product at the time, it is only of academic interest. When the need is great, then you take cognisance of the product, the vendor, the bargains and the offers.

It is naïve of solicitors to think that image is of no consequence to them and their services. If there is a monopoly, then image is largely irrelevant – the purchaser has no choice. In fact, the opposite is the case: the legal services market-place is becoming more competitive and cut-throat and law firms must look to their image as part of the business of acquiring business.

4.2.1 The image from within

An important exercise is to examine the image that your firm has of itself, that is, in the eyes of the partners and staff. This can be done by a simple questionnaire or as part of a training meeting or even a section or department discussion. This can usefully be combined with a survey of attitudes and beliefs about client care, to give a snapshot view of the present understanding of the concept. Such a survey can be conducted at every level in the firm, with opinions being sought from the managing partner as well as the newest trainee. (Details of a range of questions for such a survey are shown below.)

The results of the survey will be useful in constructing a programme of development for client care. The opinions, misapprehensions and reservations educed can be used as starting-points for training sessions. If you are not able to formalise client care training to such an extent, then the material gathered will still be very helpful in forming a base from which to stimulate further discussions towards improving client care.

Useful information can also be gathered about the image of a particular department within a firm. The results can be very helpful in improving interdepartmental relations and tightening up on levels of cooperation and cross-servicing. The exercise should include departments such as financial services, post-rooms and archiving as well as the normal legal divisions.

Questions for the survey or as starters for discussion could include:

(a) How do you believe our clients see this firm? What words would they choose to describe it?

(b) How do you see this firm? What words would you choose to describe it?

The words that might be used to describe the firm could include any of the following:

busy	overwhelming	modern	overpriced
large	expensive	classy	hi-tech
up-market	proficient	professional	distant
top-heavy	benevolent	Dickensian	cosy
confusing	impersonal	friendly	long-established
old-fashioned	too remote	unfriendly	unapproachable
top-class	glossy	up-market	favourite
excellent	top advisers	vast	poky

There will be many other words used as well! Many of the perceptions are quite positive and many rather negative. If these opinions are expressed under no duress, they need to be heeded. The positive aspects of the firm's image should be built upon and the negative ones rectified where possible. These activities are for promotion by senior people with the clout to make changes. The creation of a client care policy affords an excellent opportunity to institute changes for the better and everyone in the firm must play a part in making the changes stick.

The image the firm would like to have is not always reflected in reality. There may be historical, geographical, organisational or cultural reasons why this should be. Changing an organisation's image is complex and can be expensive as the ramifications become apparent. It is a long-term effect that is sometimes hard to justify in the short term. However, to survive, the firm must present itself to the advice-seeking public in the way that will attract the greatest amount of business, however that is defined. The image should be constructed to attract certain groups of clients and the firm will focus its image, its advertising and its market-place positioning with that in mind.

(c)   What do you understand by 'client care'? Do we do it? Who should do it?

(d)   Are there any aspects of this firm's operation that you believe cause concern or puzzlement to our clients?

(e)   Are there any operations or activities in the firm which are potential 'accident black spots' which could give rise to possible claims from clients?

(f)   Are there any favourite ways for dealing with clients in different circumstances, or improving client care generally?

(g)   What can our firm offer potential clients to give us a marketing edge over our competitors?

There is a belief that individual members of a firm can have little influence on its image, its culture or its policies. This is not true, provided that there are sensible and usable channels of communication which permit creative criticism and constructive suggestions. No matter what your position in the firm, you must not assume that you are only a small voice in a crowd, a small cog in a big machine. Major changes have been occasioned by perceptive and persistent junior members of staff pushing ideas and concepts to where the power lies. Any activity or factor about your firm which seems to militate against good client care practice must be brought to the attention of the client care group or a senior person with the remit to effect changes. Likewise, any ideas you have for boosting client care should be pursued.

The nub of this inquiry into internal perceptions of the firm is to ascertain whether these views are echoed by the perceptions of people outside. After all, it is those people who will buy the services and guarantee continuing prosperity.

In conducting an internal survey, it is important to emphasise that it is not an examination but an exercise in seeking real opinions and views, unbiased and open.

4.2.2   The image seen from outside

A law firm will be seen in different ways by different groups of clients. As mentioned before, the plush, glass-and-chrome city-centre offices will not suit all clients, nor will the backstreet, close-to-the-people establishment. The physical environment does play a large part in clients' perception of the firm.

A city-centre merger took the members of an old-established law firm located in an Edwardian, tree-lined square, across the centre to a purpose-built, bland concrete block of offices. Many of their clients did not like the new place, saying that the firm had lost its familiar comfort and respectability. The lawyers were the same, offering the same services but the location, and the image, were wrong.

Two issues arise here. Do changes in image help or hinder the maintenance of client loyalty? Is a positive change likely to alienate established clients? There is clearly a risk which must be taken into consideration when changes are contemplated.

The image of the firm in the public's mind is conditioned by several factors:

(a)   The firm's size.

(b)   The firm's offices. Often this is the first point of recognition to face a potential client. The firm's premises are spotted and an impression is made. It so much depends on what the client is seeking. A dingy alleyway leading to the offices may be ideal for furtive Fred the burglar, but many would be deterred by such an entrance. It is imperative for the firm to decide on its market position and find premises that are appropriate (it is recognised that this is more easily said than done!).

(c)   The firm's reputation locally, regionally, nationally or internationally.

(d)   The way the firm is reported in the press.

(e)   The way the firm advertises its services. This is the other most likely way for a potential client to come across the name of the firm, maybe whilst scanning Yellow Pages or in a relevant publication. Advertisement copywriting is outside the scope of this book, but suffice it to say that it is a powerful way of creating image. The advice of a specialist advertising agency is recommended to find the best use of funds available for publicity and advertising. Business magazines usually allow space for editorial copy that is interesting rather than merely promotional, when advertising space is bought.

(f)   The way the firm does (or does not) become involved with the community, with sponsorships or charitable works. Repute by association is a strong image builder. Many clients will be impressed by the sponsorship of cultural, artistic or sporting occasions. The programme material is a useful way of keeping the firm's name in the public eye.

(g)   The appearance of the firm's published materials and stationery. In 5.32 we will look at writing skills, but clients' response to the very paper that the writing appears on can help with image building just as much as the text itself can. An elegant, tasteful letterhead speaks volumes for the firm – a poorly copied, poorly designed head will not create a good impression.

(h)   The way the firm interacts or conflicts with other law firms.

(i)   The alliances the firm shows with major issues, local, national or international. A firm which spoke publicly and strongly on a particular green issue excited considerable business from like-minded litigants.

(j)   The way it is regarded by co-professionals such as accountants, estate agents and bankers.

4.2.3   Comparisons with other organisations

A fascinating exercise is to compare your perceptions of the firm with other commercial and service organisations. This can give rise to a range of ideas for (a) improving your image and (b) improving client care.

Try this approach. The organisations shown in figure 4.3 are all successful, but they have very different images in the public's eye.

(a)   How would you describe their image in a few words?
(b)   How would you rate them on client care, from 1 for dreadful to 7 for excellent?

Remember that this is your opinion – try to be as objective as possible.

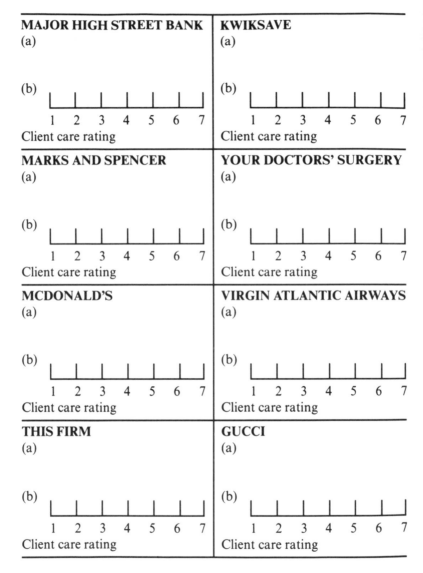

Figure 4.3   Client care rating

What can be learned from this? That the way you operate in your firm is more Marks and Spencer than Gucci, more bank than supermarket? What are the things that these organisations do really well that you do not do? What is there about these organisations that the public appreciate as creating a positive image which your firm could adopt or at least adapt?

It would be absolutely ludicrous to suggest that the partners (or even the staff) in a law firm should wear bright uniforms with merit badges for added skills as the McDonalds people do. But their cheerful attentiveness does much to improve their firm's profitability, even if it does not appeal to all. At least it appeals to their clientele! This is the whole point, that your firm must appeal to its clientele and potential clientele. There are many law firms where cheerful attentiveness is sadly lacking.

You may say that you would prefer your firm to be the Gucci or the Rolls-Royce amongst local law firms rather than be seen as the market stall with effective but very cheap goods on sale. This has to be a positive choice and one which demands work and commitment from all the partners and staff. There are law firms who do see themselves as the market stall with rapid throughput, small but numerous fees and a very busy lifestyle leading to much personal satisfaction and profitability. That too is a positive choice.

4.2.4 Process and content

A final thought on image. Once you have determined where your professional focus is to be, and you have created the right image to attract that type of client, then you have a duty to those clients to deliver the goods. It is unreasonable to dupe people into coming to your offices for quality legal advice and then to fail to meet those expectations.

This can be expressed diagrammatically as in figure 4.4.

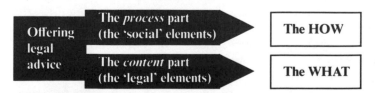

Figure 4.4   Process and content

The 'process' of offering legal advice covers all the social aspects, the reception, introductions, interviewing and the normal courtesies of business relationships. Much of the client's expectation of this part of the interaction can be assumed from his or her image of the firm, constructed from impressions and observations. It is these factors that probably drew the client to you in the first place.

The 'content' of offering legal advice is the advice itself. This is far less easy for the client to envisage before actually meeting it head-on.

It is possible to offer extremely good advice in a very uncaring and impoverished way (good content, lousy process). It is equally possible to offer dreadful advice in an elegant, pleasant and efficient manner (lousy content, good process). Your target should of course be to meet the expectations of image *and* meet the expectations of professional advice.

4.3   MARKETING AS A FACTOR IN CLIENT CARE

As marketing is directly about exciting clients' interest in the firm, it is a subject that clearly has relevance to the major purpose of this present book. (Alan Pannett covers marketing as a topic for law firms in *Managing the Law Firm* in the Legal Practice Handbook series.)

There are three fundamental concepts in marketing that have a direct and important bearing on client care: the marketing triangle, the marketing mix and the SWOT analysis.

The marketing triangle is illustrated in figure 4.5. Any change to law firms in competition with yours is likely to affect your firm and your clients. You may lose some clients, you may gain some; you may have to fight harder for business if your competitors start to offer services that previously had been just yours; you may need to import extra talent to combat incursions into your areas of work; you may have to increase the quality of your service and of your client care. You will need to keep a canny weather eye open on competitors' changes – they are unlikely to tell you of plans for capturing your clients! One way to encourage the loyalty of your clients is to be more proactive in your contacts. Speak to them before they speak to you; keep in touch with immediate past clients to have your name fresh in mind should new matters arise that you could take on.

4.3.1 The marketing triangle

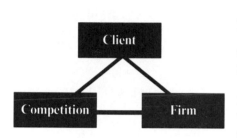

Marketing is a complex and detailed operation, but it can be simplified to a set of three essentials, and the way they interrelate.

It is crucial to understand the relationships in the triangle, to monitor any changes and to manage the relationships to your advantage.

Figure 4.5 The marketing triangle

The corollary of these points is that any changes your firm makes will be eagerly watched by the competition with an eye for stepping in to any gaps or strengthening their range of services to make you fight for your increased share of the market.

You must also watch the market. The regional client base can change with industrial expansion (or contraction – both need legal support), with new housing, transportation or commercial projects. Your image must be correct, your quality of service and client care must be correct to meet these new challenges.

4.3.2 The marketing mix

Marketing has been defined as having the right product (goods or services) at the right price, in the right place, in the right packaging and with the right promotion (see figure 4.6).

Examine your organisation in the light of these five Ps. Have you got it right? Your clients will certainly expect you to have it right. Peters and Austin do not include any of these as such in their recipe for excellence, but it is implicit in their writings that you will have given all of them much thought. What they would add is a sixth P – perfect client care (no apologies if this seems contrived – but it is an important point!).

1. Right **PRODUCT**

2. Right **PRICE**

3. Right **PLACE**

4. Right **PACKAGING**

5. Right **PROMOTION**

These are the very points being made in this book, that you have to attract your client with the perfect marketing mix.

It is reckless to believe that marketing is a technique that only applies to consumer products such as cars, washing machines and soup!

Figure 4.6   The marketing mix

4.3.3   The SWOT analysis

Given that there are forces at work inside and outside every organisation that may help or hinder its success, and given that every organisation has its good points and its bad points, there is a need for careful analysis of these factors in order to help determine a marketing strategy.

	Strengths	Weaknesses
Internal factors		

	Opportunities	Threats
External factors		

Figure 4.7   SWOT analysis

The SWOT analysis (figure 4.7) is a favourite marketing tool and a powerful one for helping determine client care policy and practices. It can be used directly on client care as a concept as evidenced within the firm. This will give strong clues about developments, whether to build on existing strengths or remedy apparent weaknesses. It will also show what the world outside needs in terms of client care, the opportunities for extension and increasing the client base or the threats looming large over the future. Opportunities need to be grasped rapidly, threats can destabilise and you therefore need defences.

4.4 THE PHYSICAL ENVIRONMENT

Reflect for a moment on those places you have visited where you felt entirely comfortable. What are the component parts of the feeling of comfort?

(a) Warmth in the sense of physical temperature as well as the ambient feeling of welcome and well-being.

(b) Comfortable furniture.

(c) The right amount of privacy for the occasion.

(d) Access to refreshments if needed and toilet and washroom facilities.

(e) No pressure to conform to rules and social mores that you do not understand.

(f) People around you who do not threaten or compromise you.

(g) A sense of time under control and absence of rush and hassle.

(h) Decor that does not intrude into your consciousness and furnishings that enhance the situation.

(i) No obtrusive noises or smells, no interruptive scurrying about or causes of agitation.

Although this could adequately describe you being asleep in bed at night, it should also describe the reception, meeting and interviewing facilities you offer your clients. Particularly in the case of individual clients, visiting a solicitor is fairly low on most people's list of fun occupations. They will be coming to see you because they cannot handle the matter themselves – it is an anxious time.

Recognising the necessity for personal physical comfort when dealing with clients is an important aspect of client care. Conversation will be enhanced, openness fostered and a stronger relationship will be created when the client is feeling comfortable with his or her surroundings. The techniques of eliciting the correct information are covered elsewhere in this book but they are made easier through being in the right environment.

Chapter Five

Communications and Relationships

This is the longest chapter in the book and is organised in a different fashion from the others. In effect, it is an alphabetical listing of a very wide range of client care concepts, techniques and procedures. Each item is dealt with fully and is cross-referenced where necessary. Some will refer back to previous text and you may find it helpful to go back and read that piece again to set the idea in context.

The list of items is extensive but they have all proved very effective for someone somewhere – they *are* tried and tested. You may find some of these items less applicable in your firm because of its size, structure, resources, culture or tradition. Some ideas you may have tried and tested already, in which case you can extend them further or try a new angle. Some ideas will need backing from the managing partner but others are applicable immediately by everyone.

Even if your firm has a long tradition of client care and its own proven track record, the overlying concepts may be flexible enough for you to pick up a few new ideas that you can use with a change or two. Check all the ideas. They are all relevant to the principal theme of improving client care and consequently encouraging the growth of your firm and you with it.

5.1 ACCOUNTS DESK

Many clients find it embarrassing to discuss the financial aspects of their account in anything other than extreme privacy. A separate accounts desk where talk and analysis can take place privately with finance officers will avoid the problems of exposing a client's payment for services as a public matter. Clients do call in to query accounts or plead poverty, and the reception area is not the place to air views and badger for payments!

5.2   AGE DIFFERENCES

I did mention at the end of 2.1.2 the idea of the client often feeling happier to interact with a counsellor of similar outlook, style, gender, age and values. It is a sign of age, they say, when policemen and doctors look too young to be real! It can also apply to lawyers, particularly when older clients see a marked difference in age between themselves and 'youthful' solicitors. It should not matter one iota, but it does matter if there is a feeling of unease in the mind of the client.

Perceptions of life and changing cultural values do create generation gaps. They are hard to bridge. 'I liked old Mr Hardcastle, *he* understood what I meant, he remembered the war, he knew me!' is difficult to overcome when you have only been with the firm five minutes.

It may be possible for an older lawyer to deal with the matter if you perceive strain developing in the relationship which you believe is caused by age differences. Client care involves the removal of discomfort in the relationship, even if it is not a matter for concern in the eyes of the solicitor personally.

A note of caution – many people are aware of, and offended by, what they describe as 'ageism', discrimination on grounds of age. This is particularly felt by older people who hate being fobbed off as of no concern because they have reached a certain age. Generalisation on matters of age is dangerous and must be avoided. The most cutting comment is, 'What do you expect at your age?' and can apply equally to young and old. Young people should never make generalised comments about the elderly; older people should never make generalised comments about the young. Those are the ways towards barriers to understanding, mutual trust and respect.

(See also 5.21 on ethnic differences and 5.23 on gender differences.)

5.3   ASSERTIVENESS AND AGGRESSION

It is important to distinguish between 'assertiveness', 'non-assertiveness' and 'aggression'.

(a)   Assertive behaviour communicates a feeling of self-respect and a sense of respect for others. It should lead to good feelings in both parties resulting in a 'win-win' situation. It is well thought-out, honest and direct, and leads to success without creating ambiguity in relationships. It is presenting our wants, needs and rights as being of equal worth to those of others.

(b)   Non-assertive behaviour communicates a feeling of non-worth, of inadequacy, inferiority and inability to cope. It helps to create 'win-lose' situations and is likely to cause ambiguity in relationships. It permits the wants, needs and rights of others to dominate and is the style of the victim, not the victor.

(c)   Aggressive behaviour communicates a feeling of disrespect and superiority by disallowing choice in others. It can generate feelings of anger, violence and guilt and is rarely appropriate behaviour, as it moves towards an 'I win, you lose' situation by force. It puts down the wants, needs and rights of others and indeed can violate the rights of others.

Assertion is therefore the style of self-expression that allows you to stand up for your basic human rights whilst allowing others to stand up equally for theirs. It is an expression of confidence, saying yes or no without fear or guilt. As someone who deals with the public constantly, you need to be clear in your mind about your own level of assertion when with them. Too much assertion can seem aggressive; too little can appear ineffectual and lacking in knowledge and confidence. Your client will expect you to be professional (i.e., positive, unbiased, ethical, objective and probably assertive) at all times, whilst attentive and caring.

Assertion amongst friends and colleagues can seem aggressive and may cause uncertainty about your degree of understanding and fellow feeling.

Your clients may resort to either direct or indirect aggression on occasions. This needs to be countered with assertion, certainly not with matching aggression! Many clues can be found as evidence of the different types of behaviour, whether it is you or your client exhibiting them!

(a)   Aggressive behaviour:

(i)   Verbal clues – boastfulness; much use of 'I' and 'my'; value judgments (opinions expressed as if they were facts); advice weighted with 'must' and 'ought'; blame dumped on others; use of sarcasm and humiliating criticism; stridency and shouting.

(ii)   Non-verbal clues – fast, clipped, fluent speech; staring down; pointing, table thumping and leaning forward; scowling or disbelieving facial expressions.

(b)   Non-assertive behaviour:

(i)   Verbal clues – use of vague words like 'maybe' and 'might'; self-dismissive phrases; self put-downs; apologetic and permission-seeking phrases; long convoluted sentences.

(ii)   Non-verbal clues – hesitations and throat-clearing; evasive eyes; shrugs and shuffles; whining, tremulous voice; fading sentences; false facial expressions.

(c)   Assertive behaviour:

(i)   Verbal clues – statements about feelings; constructive criticisms; no 'ought' or 'should'; clarity between opinions and facts; investigative, analytical and focused questions and comments.

(ii)   Non-verbal clues – good posture and body movements; facial expressions that are genuine; good eye contact; fluent, easy and warm speech; no jaw-grinding or unnecessary twitching.

Be careful to accept that clients may be quite nervous about calling to see you and that their behaviour patterns may be corrupted by that nervousness. You will need to assess their state of control early on in the meeting and allay any fears and misapprehensions that they may have. People may also be trying to make some personal statement by varying their normal behaviours. They may adopt a more aggressive tone when not finding things going all their own way – do not be duped into responding in like fashion. (See also 5.15 on difficult clients.)

You may be faced with a non-assertive client. You will need to find out what is causing this reticence to speak out, then the best way of overcoming the behaviour for this client. There are no hard-and-fast rules. It takes patience, smiling, careful probing and presenting yourself as absolutely to be trusted and enabling.

5.4   ASSESSMENT

Sizing up a situation and gathering in all the facts of a matter are skills that can be learnt. Assessing the client's needs and wants is often made difficult by the client not being too clear what it is that is actually wanted.

You will need to exercise several skills to elicit the purpose and intent of the client's visit:

(a)   Investigative skills – think of your favourite detective, probing for facts and ideas. You will need a similar approach.

(b)   Questioning skills – these are covered in 5.41.

(c)   Interviewing skills – these are covered in 5.28.

(d)   Using your knowledge of life and the vagaries of human nature.

(e)   Using your knowledge of law.

Assessment is like the first stage of problem solving, define the problem. This is essential before you can begin to seek solutions. Resist strongly the temptation to leap at a possible solution or way of acting without the full purpose and intended outcome very clearly in your mind (and in the client's, one hopes!). Then you can explore a range of options, choose the best having regard to all the circumstances of the case and take the required action.

5.5 BILLING AND COSTS

Often one of the most contentious areas of lawyer-client relationships, billing needs great care and attention. Bills are certainly one thing that your clients will understand! Your firm will have determined its charging-out rates according to patterns that suit the type of business and the people involved. Usually charges will be banded according to the position of the fee-earner in the firm and the seniority or otherwise of the individual within that band. They will also vary according to the matter being dealt with. Certain directly referable expenses can be charged on to the client as disbursements. The net result of these decisions will be a standard rate for the firm's work, often expressed as a universal hourly rate that is 'fair and reasonable having regard to all the circumstances of the case'.

Clients have a right to know what they are likely to be charged for work done and it is required that you should tell them at the beginning of their association with you. Equally, they will expect to receive a bill that is compatible with what they were originally told. Some commercial clients may even demand a cap on fees to be agreed up front. A major part of your care therefore is to be scrupulous in reckoning your chargeable time.

The Written Professional Standards require that solicitors give adequate advance information on costs to clients. This activity involves several important points:

(a) When taking instructions, you should tell the client how fees are calculated and what is the best possible estimate of costs for this matter. You should discuss how charges and disbursements will be met. Consider whether legal aid is available. Consider whether insurance will cover any costs.

(b) On writing to confirm instructions, record agreed fees and what is so covered. Identify any further likely costs and confirm estimates.

(c)   If the matter is contentious, inform clients that they will be liable for your costs in full regardless of any order for costs made against opponents. Inform them that they will probably be liable for opponents' costs as well if they lose and, if they win, their costs may still not be paid by the opponents.

(d)   If the client is meeting his or her own costs, promise to deliver a periodic review of costs (or an interim bill), explaining that future estimates are not simple or accurate. Explain that limits can be set.

Always check bills before they are dispatched to your clients as mistakes can occur even in the finest financial offices. Make sure you show disbursements.

Should problems arise with billing, the client deserves a swift and positive response. A disheartened or disgruntled client will rapidly become an ex-client if the dispute drags on or if the problem is not resolved. Refer clients with problems about billing to the agreed procedure for handling complaints.

5.6   BROCHURES

It is essential to have a basic brochure that explains the range of interests of your firm together with a bit of background history and maybe the names of the principals and/or heads of departments. This is excellent PR and allows clients to take away information to be read at leisure. Even the smallest firm can produce a meaningful pamphlet with important information about personalities, contact and services.

When your current brochure is revised, the new version can usefully be sent to ex-clients who might 'rejoin', as a reminder of your services and to let them know that they are not forgotten.

The wording of publicity material is very important as there is a need to produce useful and concise information in a small package. Some larger firms find it sensible to produce an insert for the house brochure describing each department in turn. These can also be used separately for that department's clients when required.

Recent relaxation in the Law Society's rules about promotional activities have broadened the scope for effective publicity material. Full-colour glossies are fine if that will appeal to your clients, or perhaps a stylish but informative two-tone job will do. Remember your image and the expectations of your client groups.

(See also 5.38 on pamphlets.)

5.7 CLIMATE

In 4.1.2 we looked at colleague care and internal climate. Undoubtedly the client will benefit from consulting with a firm where the lawyers and non-lawyers are equally content with the patterns and practices of the organisation. Feelings of frustration, irritation, non-cooperation, interdepartmental friction, personality clash or lack of motivation will often show through when speaking to the client and this does not encourage good conversation.

Climate can relate to two situations:

(a) The internal climate of the firm – the ambient atmosphere within which everyone works – will reflect in the way clients are treated.

(b) The climate of the meeting when the client is actually closeted with the lawyer. It is vital that this is conducive to good rapport right from the start. You have the tasks of putting the client at ease and of setting the standards. It is your guidance that will determine the tenor and tone of the meeting.

Start off by offering a warm and encouraging welcome. A smile and a reassuring handshake can dispel any qualms that the client may have. A coffee or tea is a useful soother. (See also 5.9.) The room you use will affect the meeting so care needs to be taken over general tidiness, comfort and privacy. (See also 5.22 on first impressions.)

Show right from the start that you have a thoroughly professional approach and that you intend to do all that is possible for the client compatible with the situation. The entire meeting must be focused on the client's problem, putting aside any problems of your own that may be troubling you.

(See 5.28 on interviewing for the next stages of the meeting.)

5.8 CLOSING FILES AND FOLLOW-UP

At least closing a file means that you have completed another job and, it is hoped, you have another contented client. However, when a client's case is finished, the final contact with the client is very important. Because there may have been a great deal of fairly close contact between your client and you over the time the task has taken to run its course, suddenly switching off that contact as soon as the task is completed can make the client feel somewhat cut adrift. (You do after all have a mass of other work to devote yourself to immediately.) The receipt of a bill (especially if it is rather higher than expected!), unaccompanied by any personal letter or message, can antagonise your client. A methodical approach will help your client and show that it is not merely a mechanical process.

(a) Check that the task has been completed to the client's satisfaction. You could telephone to ask whether the move into the new house had gone well or whether the new business was performing as expected, or whatever would be appropriate.

The conversation could include discussion of particular points which arose in the course of the transaction which might produce additional work. For example, a commercial client who performs certain types of deal on a regular basis, could be contacted to see if there was any way of running such deals more efficiently in the future. Such a call could also be used to warn the client that a bill was on its way and to explain how it was calculated (if this has not already been done).

(b) Do not delay closing a file — if the work is done and you have been paid, close it! If the account is not clear, take the appropriate actions.

(c) Write a final closing letter, even though you have little formally to say other than that you are putting the file in the archive.

It allows you to close the case on the right note. If the circumstances are appropriate, you can slip in one of the firm's general brochures to remind the client of available services and means of contact.

(d) Before filing the papers in the archive, consider whether there are any other services that this client could be offered. Return any papers that may be helpful to the client. Make a note in your diary to reconsider this file in a year's time to see if there are any services you could offer then, being the anniversary of the completion. Take care to check addresses — you do not want to send material to a previous address or to a wound-up estate!

(e) After you have closed the file, made a personal contact with the client to see that all was well, and have sent the closing letter, you still have not finished with the relationship. Always be aware of opportunities to contact past clients. The most obvious illustration is new developments, although this will not be appropriate for all clients or for all solicitors. It is important to target clients very carefully for such informative mail-shots or publicity drives, as material sent to the wrong client can be counter-productive and intrusive. Personal contact can be made on a purely social basis to remind clients of the firm's existence and range of services. If contact is maintained throughout this fallow period, you and the firm will remain in the clients' minds and, it is hoped, they will bring any new matters to you to deal with and will refer others to your (excellent) services.

5.9   COFFEE AND TEA

This is not a frivolous entry! People under stress need comfort and offering a drink of coffee or tea is a sound way to show care and to reduce tension. If you know that someone has travelled some distance or has had a fractious journey, it is courteous to offer a drink. If resources permit, a dispensing machine can be a good investment if installed near the reception area. Many modern machines are elegant and inconspicuous and actually make quite good beverages!

As a point of social correctness, note that it is wrong to assume that coffee-making is exclusively a junior or female prerogative!

5.10 COLLEAGUE CARE

This first appeared in 4.1.2 where we looked at styles of management and consequent feelings of cooperation and mutual trust. 'Colleague' can be defined as any other person working in your firm, no matter in what function. A truly caring firm will have built in as part of its ethos a belief in concern for colleagues and openness and freedom to share problems and offer help. This concern should run alongside an equal concern for clients.

A valuable process for looking at the way individuals and organisations operate between their concern for colleagues and their concern for clients is shown in figure 5.1. 'Concern' can be defined as the intent to do the very best for colleagues and clients without compromise or conflict.

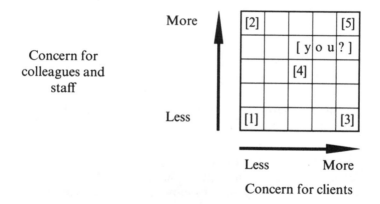

Figure 5.1 Concern for colleagues

Figure 5.1 shows that the ideal position to strive for is at point [5], where there is great concern shown for both colleagues and clients. However this may be idealistic and is certainly difficult. The typical points can be described as follows:

(a) Point [1] – an impoverished approach with virtually no concern shown for anybody. This individual needs help in developing relationships and responsibilities.

(b)   Point [2] – this individual has overwhelming care for colleagues to the detriment of the clients who are clearly seen as a
nuisance and an encumbrance. The weighting is one-way and, even
if this is a really caring and fun-loving person, there is danger looming
unless he or she develops a greater concern for client care.

(c)   Point [3] – here the weighting is all on the client even if
colleagues have to be ignored in the process. This is also a dangerous
approach as it can alienate colleagues and generate friction.

(d)   Point [4] – this is the middle-of-the-road position where the
individual is trying hard to balance the two concerns with not too
much of either. It is a better position to be in than any of the previous
three, but is not yet good enough.

(e)   Point [5] – the optimum achievement where clients and
colleagues are considered well and equally.

You will probably find amongst your present or past colleagues
examples of all these positions (or positions very close to them). You
yourself will appear somewhere on the chart, maybe not as one of
these five extreme types, but more likely around the area marked
'you?', heading towards the ideal, balancing concern for your
colleagues and for your clients.

It may be necessary on occasions to swing your approach towards [2]
or [3]. For instance, when a colleague is clearly in trouble and in need
of strong support, you may have to move closer to [2] temporarily
until the problem is resolved, even if you are rather more short and
peremptory with your clients in the process. Conversely it may be
necessary to give great attention to a client in dire need, and not be
so cooperative with colleagues whilst doing so, i.e., moving closer
towards [3]. Provided afterwards you swing your approach back to
where your colleagues normally expect to find you, the temporary
shift is acceptable. People who position themselves all over the chart
at different times are hard to live with and are disruptive of the
established patterns. It is hard to recognise whether they are in this
mode or that at any time. Clients and colleagues will find this
irritating, not knowing how to react.

Other sensible approaches to improved colleague care include:

(a)   Avoid using phrases like 'It's not my problem'. That is not a team concept!

(b)   Try to keep up to date with the activities of your colleagues and especially with their developing specialisms. Tell them about yours too.

(c)   Share ideas for developing professionalism.

(d)   Offer praise where it is due. Praise is a marvellous motivator and often absence of it demotivates. Celebrate notable victories. There is insufficient celebration in organisations. It does not take much effort to gather people together for a few minutes and share a bottle or a large fancy cake when a colleague has achieved a great triumph.

(e)   Never dictate letters at 4.30 p.m. Even secretaries have homes to go to! You might like staying around the office until the epilogue, but do not assume others will want to join you.

(f)   Seek cheques from cashiers early. They also have homes to go to.

(g)   If you are going to be away from your desk for any substantial time, tell someone where you can be contacted or when you will return. Arrange for messages to be left or picked up. If you are going to be away for some time, arrange for a deputy to speak for you.

(h)   Encourage colleagues to develop their skills and areas of knowledge. Show a creative interest in their careers.

5.11   CONVERSATIONAL STYLE

Your client will expect you to be inquisitive and persistent in your questioning, but will not expect to be subjected to the third degree! The conversational style needs to be carefully established at the beginning of the meeting. The normal courtesies of social intercourse must obtain, however demanding you choose to be. These will include:

(a)   Finding a sensible place to converse, not where there will be interruptions or other people within earshot.

(b)   Showing that you are attentive, through body posture, facial expressions and encouraging gestures. A client who feels that you are not paying attention will become disillusioned, resentful and unforthcoming.

(c)   Maintaining eye contact at the right level of continuity (a constant, staring gaze is not only very off-putting and repellent, it is also rude).

(d)   Making it quite clear which bits of the conversation are the politenesses and which bits are hard fact gathering.

(e)   Working through an agenda, even if it is only a verbal one agreed at the start of the conversation.

(f)   Ensuring that the client is comfortable with the conversation and with the environment at all times.

(See also 5.28 on interviewing style and 5.41 on questioning techniques.)

5.12   CONFIDENTIALITY

This aspect of the client-lawyer relationship need hardly be stressed. However, the client will be reassured by your reaffirming that the information received will only be used by yourself and any other colleagues or co-professionals whose expertise needs to be sought in the matter. Even if this is not strictly true (administrative and secretarial staff may have legitimate access), the client will wish to believe that confidentiality is a highly revered concept with you and with the firm.

5.13   COUNSELLING

Counselling can be defined as a means of exploring a person's problem with a view to understanding it better and helping the person towards acceptance or resolution of the problem. Counselling as so defined is not the normal role of the lawyer, but is more of a service offered by people trained in a different discipline.

There will be times when you will be working with a client who clearly needs counselling, but where you feel ill-equipped or out of your depth to deal with such a problem. There should be no difficulty in recommending the specialised and professional services of a local or national agency with relevant skills. This will be, and will be seen to be, a better piece of care than your trying to act as analyst or therapist.

There are a number of activities and actions you can take:

(a)   Arm yourself with information about the major national and local counselling agencies – there are services to cover almost every contingency. Have a list handy, with names of individuals if possible. You may already have made contact with an agency on behalf of a client, in which case you can explain their services and even effect a personal introduction.

(b)   Offer to fix an appointment for your client if that would be appropriate.

(c)   Be alert for hidden agendas – your client may be concealing facts for fear of embarrassment, ridicule or exposure. You may be able to help bring the real problem into the open.

(d)   Do not be drawn into situations you cannot handle. Explain that there are people better qualified than you are to deal with such problems and that your concern is only to offer legal advice.

5.14 COURTESY

Courtesy is defined as politeness or good manners, to include correct, elegant and caring social behaviour between individuals. It is sadly a dying practice. Clients who come to you with problems that they cannot contain themselves, to seek professional help towards resolution or avoidance, are under strain. Extending common courtesy is a great reassurance that they are with someone who recognises the need for a civilised approach and who will respect the rights and existence of another human being.

5.15 DIFFICULT CLIENTS

In *Effective Interviewing* by Helena Twist, a companion book in the Legal Practice Handbook series, the author identifies a range of things that can go wrong in interviews. The list is included here in summary with some implications for client care. Even difficult or obstreperous clients deserve care, particularly if it will reduce the aggravation and calm them down.

(a) Clients who talk too much, for whatever reason, need to be kept in check lest their time is wasted (not to mention yours!). Rambling and uncontrolled digression can cloud issues and add detail that is really not needed. Keep the client to the point – they will thank you for it eventually. Ask yourself if your behaviour has caused the client to talk excessively. Are you showing signs of indifference, apathy or boredom?

(b) Clients who talk too little may be embarrassed, pained by the topic or lacking a grasp of the discussion. You need to change the style or pace and encourage them to explain their reticence. Are you behaving in such a way that they may be intimidated, overawed or frightened? (See also 5.3 on assertiveness and aggression.)

(c) Clients may not listen, particularly if your advice is not what they wanted to hear! You may find difficulties if you are a trainee or relatively newly qualified, when your experience or depth of knowledge may be impugned. Do not become defensive, reaffirm your strengths and re-emphasise your commitment to the client's problems.

(d) Clients may withhold or doctor the truth or may present conflicting or contradictory statements. In order to give a quality service, you need to know the whole story. Do not be hesitant in asking direct questions to find the truth and the reasons for duplicity. Could it be your manner that makes the client withhold information?

(e)   Clients may become aggressive for many reasons. You will need to preempt any potential aggression by alertness for the clues mentioned in 5.3 and careful interviewing style. Aggression may be passive (by words or behaviour changes) or active (by physical assault or threatened assault). A client who resorts to aggression inevitably lose face and you will need compassion and benevolence to restore the status quo.

(f)   Clients may become highly distressed. The trauma of events or even of coming to see you, may cause a breakdown in your presence. If you are embarrassed by it, admit so to the client. No help is offered if you ignore it. Endeavour to return to calm by modifying the topic or by changing your questioning style to a more direct, less narrative style.

5.16   DISASTERS

Disasters come in two flavours – theirs and yours!

(a)   In his seminal book on counselling, *On Becoming a Person*, Carl Rogers said that to offer help you had to be totally non-judgmental (accepting the person for him or herself, warts an' all), completely empathic and always congruent in your feelings and utterances. When presented with someone else's disaster, you have to remain dispassionate and very alert to feelings and sensitivities. Empathy is feeling *with*, not feeling *for* – that is 'sympathy'. It is unlikely that you will be the first person to hear of the disaster, be it financial, matrimonial, economic or whatever. The narrative you receive will be rehearsed but nonetheless potent for that.

The skills you will need for dealing with another's disaster are:

(i)   Patience and calmness to hear out the tale.

(ii)   Guidance in steering the conversation and heading towards resolution or further activities.

(iii)   Listening and interpreting skills to sift the essential elements from the surrounding emotional embellishments.

(iv)   Ability to draw in additional resources if necessary.

(v)   Personal resolve not to take up causes for reasons other than offering legal advice.

(b)   If the disaster is caused by you or your firm, through bad advice, ill-conceived lines of action or sheer negligence, the situation is very serious. (See chapter 6 for ideas on preventing claims.) It is unlikely to be a matter for you to deal with alone, demanding support from the top. Retrieving a good client from a mess caused by a solicitor is difficult in the extreme.

5.17   DRESS

As suggested in chapter 2, there is a strong expectation that, when dealing with clients, lawyers and their staffs would be well-dressed within the current dictates of formal business fashion. This expectation applies equally to private as to business clients.

It is a matter of great curiosity and delight to see Continental professional advisers wearing summery clothes and more relaxed styles of dress, but in no way losing their professionalism or their quality of advice.

British business dress seems at times to have a certain stuffiness about it with men required to wear suits and ties on all occasions, regardless of the weather, and women being decorous and semi-formal whilst at work. However, if this is what the client expects, and it usually is, then professional advisers themselves fly against this expectation at their peril.

The problem lies in what 'well-dressed' means. There are conventions for lawyers appearing in court, although horsehair may be at the end of its days if some reformers have their way! When seeing clients at your office, you will no doubt be expected to conform with the cultural mores of your firm, maybe even having received an instruction on what will be required when you first joined. You breach those conventions and customs only if you enjoy risk-taking! The dress code may vary between establishments, with the backstreet branch dealing with furtive Fred the burglar possibly allowing a less rigorous conformity than the city-centre showpiece. The rule of thumb should be to dress, whether man or woman, in a style that would seem best to match the expectations of your client group.

5.18 EMOTIONS

Helena Twist, in *Effective Interviewing*, speaks of 'emotional contagion'. A situation may suddenly occur when you experience a flush of emotion having possibly tuned in to your client's wavelength so well that you are picking up some of the anxiety or tension felt by the client. You will need to distance yourself from these feelings swiftly but that involves identifying what is the cause.

Everyone has areas of belief or sets of values which are hard to express and discuss. Emotion can be triggered by hearing someone else struggling with them. More difficult are those values or beliefs that you just cannot bear to talk about or where you have absolute, deep, personal experiences or views – your personal 'sticking points'. These highly sensitive emotional barriers can be around such subjects as abortion, child abuse, personal loss or euthanasia. All that is said in this paragraph relates equally to solicitors and clients.

An otherwise very level-headed senior adviser had suffered enormous personal trauma and great grief on the death of her parents. She was not able to confront this pain within herself and certainly could not cope with the subject of great personal loss when dealing with clients or colleagues. It was her sticking point and she had to abandon conversations whenever the topic arose.

You may be confronted by outbursts of emotion from a client if you touch a raw spot, mentioning (even in all innocence) a subject that is immensely, personally sensitive. You will need patience, tolerance and understanding in measure to offer the care necessary to contain the situation. Never resort to the 'I do know what you are feeling' response. It creates more emotion than it cures even if it sounds empathic. The owner of the grief or fear cannot conceive of anyone else understanding it or appreciating its enormity. If necessary, suggest professional help from elsewhere (see also 5.13 on counselling.)

5.19   ENGLISH LANGUAGE

Your clients will expect to understand what you are saying (a very legitimate expectation!). However, your education, training and experience may well have given you an intellectual edge over many clients, not to mention a stronger, more professional and legal-technical vocabulary. When talking or writing to clients, remember that they have a right to understand. Couch your messages in such a way that the language is unambiguous and straightforward. Use simple phrases and words whenever possible. Avoid circumlocutory prolixity and periphrastic loquaciousness! Do not, however, oversimplify to the point where the precise legal meaning or sense is lost. There will be occasions when you will need the technical word rather than the colloquial or lay one, the uncommon rather than the commonplace.

Your choice of words must also be tempered by your knowledge of the recipient of the message, whether written or spoken. For each occasion, you must find a middle course between pomposity and condescension, between legalese and noddy-language. The English language is probably the most flexible in the world and it is rare that a correct meaning cannot be expressed in a precise way that is neither overly complex nor understated and simplistic. Your clients should never have to ask what this or that communication means.

The English language is your major resource. It is the mechanism by which you conceptualise, rationalise, organise and communicate your professional skills and knowledge. Effective speaking and writing involves using this resource well.

(See also 5.29 on jargon and 5.32 on letters.)

5.20   ENTHUSIASM

When examining what the client might expect from a personal point of view, I said there would be a hope that he or she would be made to feel important and that the lawyer would be attentive and caring. You will be the first to admit that a troublesome client appearing on spec for advice at 4.00 p.m. on Friday afternoon is not your favourite idea. Whenever you see a client, regardless of the inconvenience, the other pressures, the impossible time schedules, the queue of anxious litigants, the impending court appearance, your client is still your client and you will be expected to be enthusiastic about helping. Your client probably believes that you are there twiddling your thumbs, waiting for someone to call to relieve the boredom. Not so.

There will be times when you have to say, 'No, not now'. This can be done with care and with consideration. Always fix an alternative date and time for a meeting, preferably as soon as possible. Be keen to help. It will not hurt your client to realise that you are a busy, popular and sought-after lawyer, and that, in spite of pressures, you are still enthusiastic about the matter in hand.

5.21 ETHNIC AND OTHER DIFFERENCES

There are three main areas for consideration in examining the avoidance of racial and sexual discrimination. First there is the promotion of equal opportunities in employment in solicitors' firms (and implications for colleague care practices); second, the compliance or otherwise with requests for lawyers of a particular gender or racial group; third, ways of working with clients from minority racial groups. These will be looked at in turn.

5.21.1 Equal opportunities

There is a clear obligation on firms to adopt a positive and effective policy on equal opportunities in firms. The Race Relations Act 1976 and the Sex Discrimination Act 1975 (as amended) are the relevant Acts. They identify direct and indirect discrimination:

(a) Direct discrimination is where a person is treated less favourably because of sex, colour, race, nationality or ethnic or national origins.

(b) Indirect discrimination is where a condition is applied to all but where a person is from a group proportionately less able to comply because of sex, colour, race, nationality or ethnic or national origins

Many organisations have produced codes of practice and equal opportunities policies in line with the requirements of these Acts. If your firm has not yet done so, it should make a start right away, ignoring any grumbles that it will take time and money. Having an equal opportunities policy ensures that your firm will be able to recruit and keep the very best professional staff available, regardless of gender or racial origins and thereby offer a better service to clients.

The Law Society booklet, *Equal Opportunities in Solicitors' Firms* is one such production and it offers examples of appropriate wording for firms to use in stating their policy. The policy should cover positive action for women, ethnic minorities and the disabled. A general statement should declare:

> This firm is committed to provide equal opportunities in employment. This means that all job applicants and employees will receive equal treatment regardless of sex, marital status, race, colour, nationality, ethnic or national origins or disability.

In terms of colleague care, the vital words are 'all . . . employees will receive equal treatment'. This should not only be clearly stated but must also be carried out.

5.21.2   Requests for specific lawyers

It may be that your client asks for an adviser of a particular gender or racial group, or asks that you instruct a barrister of a particular gender or racial group. You have a duty to discuss such requests with your client to establish whether the demand is made on purely discriminatory grounds or whether there is a reasonable belief that a particular class of adviser or barrister might be more effective in the circumstances of the particular case. If the request appears to be a discriminatory one, you should consider whether it is proper to continue to act if your client refuses to modify the request.

The above point is taken from the Law Society booklet, *The Race Report* (1989), and helps to clarify the stated principle:

> Solicitors must not discriminate on grounds of race or sex in their professional dealings with clients, employees, other solicitors, barristers or other persons.

A number of groups, such as the Society of Black Lawyers, are working on policy statements and codes of practice for dealing with such matters as 'internal' discrimination. This in itself is regrettable, as it indicates that there is a need for such codes and policies.

5.21.3 Working with clients from ethnic and other minorities

The principle stated in 5.21.2 declares that solicitors shall not discriminate in dealing with clients. That accepted, there are occasions when the cultural or belief framework of your client will make it difficult to relate comfortably or with any level of commonality in communicating and understanding. Some organisations have taken a line on discrimination that is wider than the law demands and is undoubtedly more accepting in the class of person deemed to have a right to be treated equally. One such list includes 'a person's race, colour, ethnic origin, nationality, sex, marital status, sexual orientation, disability, creed, trade union activities, political beliefs, age, class or caring responsibilities'. This demands a wide span of knowledge and tolerance for legal advisers and subsumes a complete lack of any bias or prejudice within the general abilities of the adviser.

You will need to be aware of the possibility of clashes over culture, faith or belief. In order to offer a comprehensive service to your client you may need to secure additional advice. It may be necessary to secure the services of an interpreter (see 5.28 on interpretation service).

Some literature may be available in your area to assist with dealing with ethnic minority groups, particularly where racial societies or groups exist and where community cultural centres are established. Groups like Citizens Advice Bureaux sometimes offer guidance on matters such as languages, cultures and Asian patronymics, for example. Local law centres who often deal with ethnic and other minorities may have material on these client groups. It pays to research resources in advance, in order to be well-prepared and thus able to offer a good service to all clients.

A comprehensive research paper from the CAB, *Citizens Advice Bureaux Service to Black Clients* by Jean Ellis (NACAB 1992), points out a number of important facts of interest to lawyers. It suggests that black clients are likely to be attracted to service providers where black people are known to be working; that ethnic minority populations need to be sensitively targeted with offers of services, particularly those groups who are faced with the greatest cultural difference barriers; publicity material should be produced in minority languages; positive contact with ethnic groups can result in more approaches by clients; black clients do not automatically wish to see black advisers; they may be happier on occasions to speak with someone with an understanding of the cultural issues. Many of these issues can be translated to clients from all minority groups.

Other research on services for minority groups suggests further ideas which could bear on the client care services offered by law firms, particularly in city areas. Many people from minority groups do not fully understand the law services on offer, or the roles of lawyers; they may fear partiality or class or caste barriers; they may fear being lumped together as 'foreigners', 'West Indians' or 'Asians' without reference to the many and diverse backgrounds and cultures from which they come; they may believe that the lawyers could not possibly understand their problems not being from the same culture; they may fear that their accents will be ridiculed or misunderstood; they may fear that the linguistic difficulties will be too much to cope with; they may fear 'official' probing into their affairs. These considerations should be accommodated in any discussions about services to clients in areas with large ethnic groupings.

5.22   FIRST IMPRESSIONS

First impressions need to be examined from the points of view of both the client and the firm. Both viewpoints are critical in starting a client-lawyer relationship on the right footing.

5.22.1   Your view of the client

Writers on interviewing and other social interactions claim that when a person enters your orbit for the first time, the immediate impression you receive will colour the predominant views you have of that person for a long time. Recruitment interviewers speak of, and warn you against, the 'halo effect', the belief that a perfectly groomed, well-spoken individual will have only perfectly groomed habits, beliefs and behaviours. This is patently not true! (Note also that the person who appears at first glance to be run down and disreputable is not inevitably also run down in spirit or personal courage.) Similarly there is danger in believing that because Jack runs up the stairs two at a time, he will do everything in great bounds and at high speed.

In offering a caring but professional approach to your clients, you must be wary of making snap judgments about people based on first impressions. This is possibly less of a danger with business clients than with private clients who may be coming with major problems or emotional strains and thus not at their best. Do be aware though that the business client may be exhibiting a great urbanity and sang-froid but covering a duplicitous and devious intent!

Allow yourself time to create an accurate view of the client. Allow yourself time to modify or totally reverse the first impressions if that be the case. Do not let those first reactions become unalterable convictions.

5.22.2   The client's view of you

Clients are very typical of the population at large and are prone to the same irrational beliefs and interpretations. When a potential client approaches your establishment to see if there is good reason for using your services as opposed to the law firm down the road, the situation is similar to your standing in a French town square and trying to decide which café to enter for your croissants and coffee. Some of your analysis will be considered and logical, some will be emotional and some determined by past experience and 'technical' knowledge as both tourist and coffee drinker. The probability is that you will choose the café that best fits your remembrance of previous cafés, tinged with the overall aesthetic/hygienic/Gallic/welcoming appeal. You could of course be wrong because the one on the corner sells the best coffee and croissants even if it is scruffy and full of Gauloise smoke!

The wondering client is still trying to choose. If it is the first time a law firm has been approached, the final decision will be less clearly justifiable and will be based more on emotions and gut-feel. This will be tinged with the overall aesthetic/professional/legal/welcoming appeal as with you and the French café. However, and it is a big however, once the decision is made, the first impressions received on coming in may well be the lasting impressions. This means that your visual and social emanations, your organisational aura, must be exactly what you would hope your clients are seeking. They must receive good feelings about your firm *from the first moments* of the relationship. This encompasses the first interactions between the client and the receptionists, the administrative and secretarial staff and the lawyer. The most important in terms of first impressions is the contact with the receptionist who carries a great responsibility for creating the right image and the right indication of what is to follow.

The first impressions the client has of you will include your manner, greeting, smile, voice, appearance and deportment. It also includes impressions of your desk! A loose, untidy heap of papers ('open-cast' filing!) may suggest a personal untidiness or excess pressure, either of which may lead the client to believe that you are not fully in control. Maybe you are too busy to put your best efforts into the client's business?

Lawyers are notoriously unpunctual (but always with some plausible excuse) and this lack of courtesy can be most exasperating for clients. Do try to be precisely on time for scheduled meetings — this is an integral part of the image.

(See also 5.42 on reception skills.)

5.23   GENDER DIFFERENCES

There are occasions when a client may feel less vulnerable or more at ease when speaking with an adviser of the same gender. If this can be arranged, then it should be done. Surveys have revealed that women often feel more at ease when visiting lawyers if the receptionist is female and the adviser is also female. Great care must be taken not to fall foul of the very specific laws on discrimination. This topic is dealt with in greater depth in 5.21.

5.24 HIERARCHY

The shape and size of the firm can have considerable influence on approaches to client care. A range of organisational 'shapes' exist which either help or hinder client care:

Figure 5.2   Tall

(a)   The tall, role-riddled firm (figure 5.2) has a multiplicity of hierarchic layers and consequently a long chain of command. Motivation tends to be coercive with each level of management seeking its own control over more junior staff. Information flow is slow and over-edited at each stage. This leads to great difficulty in installing new systems and people in the firm have to do too much asking and too little initiating. Client care tends to be stifled and cash-flow and systems are the powerful regulators.

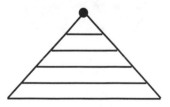

Figure 5.3   Traditional

(b)   The traditional, task-oriented, triangular firm (figure 5.3) has fewer levels of hierarchy but there are still chains of command that can interrupt free-flowing communications from top to bottom and vice versa. Client care tends to be done at the lower levels as the upper levels have less contact with clients, being more concerned with day-to-day control. Company policies, including that of client care, tend to have different interpretations at different levels of the hierarchy and in different departments.

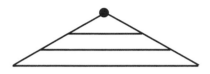

Figure 5.4   Flat

(c)   The flat, team-cultural firm (figure 5.4) still has a recognisable and effective head, but far fewer levels of hierarchy and shorter chains of command. Flow of information is well controlled and most people have a say in organisational matters. Individuals tend to have a greater span of control and more project or team involvements, but more responsibility and a closer link to the top. Client care can be effective because everyone has a strong commitment to corporate success.

Figure 5.5   Existential

(d)   The existential firm has very few if any hierarchic levels and very short chains of command. Motivation is through stressing personal experience and responsibility, recognition of effort, effective teamwork and high levels of involvement in all company affairs. Information flow is efficient and multi-directional and people are kept well in touch with each other's work through informative and personal interactions. As individuals have a great deal of independence and freedom to pursue their own styles, client care can be full and effective and a crucial part of the firm's ethos.

Whatever shape and size your firm is, the success of the client care programme will depend ultimately on unflagging support and commitment from the very top. Without that, motivation to pursue the client care policies and practices will evaporate and the scheme will founder. If your managing partner is not wholly convinced of the value of improved client care, show him or her this section and suggest that some company reorganisation is long overdue!

5.25   HOUSE STYLE

House style has two main aspects, both of which have a strong bearing on client care. First there is the physical appearance of all the printed matter that is produced for publicity, administration and communication; second is the style of performance of the firm.

5.25.1   Printed material and corporate image

Part of the earlier analysis of image suggested that it was important to have an effective and crisp house style for all printed matter that was representative of the firm and its perceived place in the market. A corporate livery, logo and style identify you amongst the others, they make your written communications instantly recognisable and they give the clients a format of communicating to which they can readily relate.

One firm that had recently been created by the merging of three smaller partnerships, decided for reasons of economy (false as it happens!) to use up the three stocks of old stationery alongside a newly and swiftly designed plain letterhead. The clients were unutterably confused and the staff were aggravated by the number of times they had to explain the confusion. In such a situation, a complete revamping of the entire range of documents would have been far more effective in consolidating the status of the new firm and reducing confusion and distress caused by an inconsistency of style and format.

Many competent PR firms will assist with the design of corporate stationery (at a cost) and will advise on colour, lettering fonts and layout as well as the design of logos and brochures.

A reorganised firm had a new design created for them which involved embossing the new logo on the letterheads rather than printing it. The effect was startling and elegant with its clean lines, but it photocopied as completely blank!

5.25.2   The style of operating

This is far harder to quantify or categorise. Operational style depends on a number of important factors:

(a)   The preferred style of the managing partner or of all the partners, will frequently impose itself on the firm and may well affect the areas of organisational analysis we discussed in chapter 4 under 'patterns of organisation'. These preferences will be determined by the partners' skills, experiences, areas of knowledge, cultural background and personality.

(b)   The way functions of operational management are distributed amongst the partners or allocated to functional committees will affect the style of the firm. Individual partners may take on responsibility for specific tasks such as recruitment or training and their own styles will be reflected in the commitment and effort used to address these non-fee-earning but important managerial activities.

(c)   The chosen market niche may determine style of operation in order correctly to meet the clients' expectations. The style of approach that furtive Fred the burglar will expect will differ from the style sought by (and delivered to) the business client with a multimillion-pound takeover in mind.

(d)   The firm's approach to information technology can affect the style. Few firms retain the Dickensian image of high desks, starched collars and endless handwritten scribblings. Smaller firms may choose to preserve their long-established air of genteel respectability and personalised attention, whilst others may embrace IT with a consuming passion. Undoubtedly a technologically brilliant service would seem to the client to denote a matching sparkle and brilliance in legal advice.

(e)   The firm's perceived role in the community or society in general will affect the style. The distinctly up-market firm may choose to appear aloof and cerebral, others may choose to be involved, sporting and approachable. This may also apply to individual lawyers within the firm – it is a profession that attracts as many 'types' as you can shake a stick at!

(f)   Does the firm's culture determine the style of operating or is it the other way round? Chicken or egg? Newcomers will need to identify and espouse the cultural and stylistic parameters very soon after appointment in order to fit in comfortably with the firm's way of working.

5.26   INTERFACES

Any meeting between you and a client can be described as an interface (a word beloved of computer types when referring to the linking of any two systems). The firm has a variety of interfaces with the client, both collectively and on an individual basis, which can be put into three categories:

(a)   The primary interfaces are the face-to-face and voice-to-voice meetings – the interviews and telephone calls. These are under your direct control and can greatly affect the quality of client care. The techniques of interviewing are discussed at 5.28 and telephone style at 5.43.

(b)   The secondary interfaces are also under your direct control, being the various examples of advertising and correspondence. Advertisements of whatever type, be they ads in the accepted sense, editorial copy, promotional brochures, sponsorship write-ups and information or notices displayed at your premises, are ambassadors of your service. They should emphasise your client care policies as well as the quality and breadth of your service. Letters, faxes, memos and other correspondence convey powerful images about your way of operating. They not only indicate your interest in working with the client, but speed and efficiency of response speak volumes about your back-up systems and administrative competence.

(c)   The least controllable are the second-hand interfaces where your repute and efficiency of operation are passed on by word of mouth. Such vicarious exchanges can damage you anywhere and at any time if a disgruntled client spreads news of the disgruntlement, which can then be spread on further through other random meetings. Equally, a satisfied client can tell of the satisfaction and that in turn can spread further, giving you some good, free publicity.

A neighbour chatted over the fence about a problem he was having with his solicitor and the preparation of papers for a divorce. The gist of the complaint was that time was edging by and the other party's solicitor was getting pushy. His man seemed to be doing nothing. Eventually he gave up trying to urge matters forward, and suffered unnecessary difficulties as a result. He was heard several times in the local pub giving forth about the ineffectual solicitor and was clearly getting through to his audience who were nodding in sympathy. No doubt his cronies passed on the story amongst their friends and neighbours and a fair clutch of potential clients was lost forever as a result of one piece of prevarication, whether it was justified or not.

On the other hand, let me tell you about this fantastic little restaurant I have found where they do extraordinary things with lamb and redcurrants. They never advertise but they . . .

5.27   INTERPRETATION SERVICE

It may be necessary to make special arrangements for clients who do not have English as their first or preferred language. If the need is great, you will need to establish an effective interpretation service, possibly using volunteers. Most city centres have community services bureaux who can provide information about help with the languages like Gujarati, Hindi, Bengali or Cantonese. Other sources of help include university or college languages departments, embassies and legations, international trade or cultural organisations or professional interpretation and translation bureaux.

Services to ethnic minority groups who may be under-represented by lawyers from their own background will welcome the announcement of legal services catering for their language. Notices to this effect can be posted on your premises or advertised in local papers. Pamphlets in such languages can be produced using the same resources as mentioned above. These should be available at reception or in community centres as appropriate.

Now that the EC is a reality, there is an increasing need to be able to operate in any of the European languages. It is a sad fact that most English people pursue their arrogant belief that speaking with foreigners is effective if done slowly and loudly in English. It is not so! Even small law firms can become involved with European matters when it will be necessary to have proficient foreign language speakers on hand to translate, interpret and advise. Many organisations, legal and non-legal, have over the past few years advised British companies to be ready for European trading openness from 1993 onwards. What has your firm done to meet these new and important international challenges?

5.28 INTERVIEWING

In Helena Twist's excellent book in this series *Effective Interviewing*, she outlines the essential characteristics of a good interview from the first preparations to the closing sentences. It would be presumptuous to try to summarise the book here, indeed unnecessary, as it stands as a source of study on its own. The following points are taken from the book and from other sources, and are looked at with particular reference to client care practices in the law office.

The entire process of interviewing clients should be an occasion to exhibit the greatest care and concern for a number of reasons:

(a)   The client will have a great deal of information to pass on to you in order for you to advise how the problem might be resolved or prevented. The time available for this is limited (if by nothing else, then by the client's ability to meet your charge-out rates). You will need to exercise good chairing and questioning skills and good agenda observation.

(b)   Some preparation is necessary. It is discourteous and irresponsible to welcome a client and have absolutely no idea what you intend to do at the meeting. If it is a first meeting then you should at least give yourself some key objectives to assist your own trains of thought and thereby aid the client also. These might be:

(i)   to establish a good rapport with the client;

(ii)   to find out the client's expectations and hopes;

(iii)   to gather in sufficient information to make a realistic preliminary diagnosis and sound plans for further action;

(iv)   to offer sound legal advice;

(v)   to explain the fee structure and payment methods and any administrative details.

If you have met the client before then preparation is even more essential. There are previous papers to review and matters to report from these – especially reports of progress and fulfilment of promised actions since the last meeting. You can also ask the client to do some preparation. Anticipate what documents you might need to look at and ask for them to be brought along. This proactive approach to meetings can save time and will create a good impression.

(c)   It is important to allocate enough time to the interview and preferably at a time to suit your client. If for some reason you are held up and cannot be ready exactly on time, ensure that your secretary keeps the client well informed. Receptionists and secretarial staff should be informed of possible arrivals, should note the times of interviews and endeavour to guide the client to the right place for the right time. On occasions they will need to be very tactful and conciliatory when timings slip and the client becomes anxious or even angry. Never say things such as 'Typical! She is always running late!' Be apologetic when appropriate but firm in your willingness to help. There will always be occasions when schedules are ruined by unforeseen events. Clients should not be fussed with the firm's internal problems – they are problem-laden enough themselves already. Care must be taken to ensure their comfort. Every courtesy must be extended to them until the adviser is able to see them.

(d)   The location for the interview must be carefully chosen. Many firms use a small room set aside for interviewing. This has several advantages, especially for the client:

(i)   There is less likelihood of interruptions or phone calls affording the two of you a clear run at the problem. Calls arriving during an interview should in any case be intercepted and dealt with by the secretary or clerk acting as keeper of the watch. The simple expedient of a 'Vacant/Free' sign will preclude colleagues from barging in.

(ii)   The room is likely to be tidier than your desk! It must not be allowed to become the junk-room as so often happens in firms. There is no advantage whatever in asking a client to sit in a room that is full to the eaves with old files or where cardboard boxes cover half the floor.

A young delinquent client was interviewed in a room where piles of papers littered the table and floor and he noticed with delight that there was a fat file about a light-fingered friend of his amongst the mess. Later that night he broke into the offices and walked off with that and several other files about people he knew. He would not have thought of the idea if the place had been properly tidied and maintained.

(iii)   Privacy is assured, with no possibility of anyone else overhearing. This may be of far greater comfort and importance to the client than it is to you.

(iv)   The furniture can often be arranged in a more suitable way than having to sit either side of a desk, which can place the client at a distinct disadvantage. Sitting at an angle beside one another suggests a greater commitment to the relationship than sitting directly opposite in an inquisitorial manner. A table to one side can still be used for notes and papers without it forming the physical and psychological barrier that a desk would.

(e)   The interview must have a clear pattern. This is the responsibility of the interviewer and can be structured as an agenda, albeit an informal or merely verbally agreed one. Having an agreed pattern will help the client to see the way forward and to assess the progress of the meeting. For a second or subsequent interview, you can compile an agenda and send it to the client ahead of the meeting. This will show that you have the client's matter in mind and that you have taken the trouble to think well ahead, thus saving time and money and preventing possible confusion over the purpose of the meeting.

Your interview will probably go through several stages:

(i)   The opening shots include the greeting, the inconsequential setting-at-ease conversation that helps to establish the relationship and the laying down of ground rules and agreeing agenda. The first few minutes of any conversation are crucial for creating the right climate, clarifying that the purpose is well-understood by all concerned and allowing each party to assess and evaluate the other's approach, demeanour and style. This is particularly important for the client, who may be in a very strange environment and rather worried about what to expect.

One particularly effective legal interviewer gives herself two minutes precisely to open the meeting through trivial chat, usually about something seasonal and whilst standing at the window. After a surreptitious glance at her watch she says, 'Right, let's start on the real business in hand, shall we? Won't you sit down here?' and the meeting swings straight into gear and takes off immediately. She explains that those two minutes allow them both to get used to the other's voice, the acoustic of the room and enables each to eye the other up and down before the important talk begins. It works well.

(ii)   Gathering the facts of the problem and the issues involved come next with the client telling the details, encouraged and opened up by careful questioning and effective listening.

(iii)   Once you have established the broad outline of the problem, you can seek clarification on specific points that are still not clear. Once the whole problem has been properly described and you are content that you understand it, you should summarise your understanding and ask the client for agreement or correction as appropriate.

(iv)   Confirm who will be handling the case and who can be contacted if any problems arise; what you will be doing in the matter and what you would like the client to do; what the likely time-scale is and information on costs (see also 5.5 on billing and costs). Offer advice to the client or explain what the next stages are. Your actions must depend on the client's wishes even if you would choose to modify these in the light of the information you have received. Always explain why you are trying to change the client's mind.

At subsequent meetings, inform your client of any progress or delays; explain important documents; advise on any personnel changes and revised costs or estimates.

(v)   The close of the interview is as important as the start. You will need to leave time for any last questions before you finally summarise by indicating what might happen next, and by when. It may be necessary to remind the client about fees.

(f)   The style of the interview needs careful analysis. The key word in offering a sound service to your clients is 'honesty'. You have a responsibility to be up-front with your clients and to be honest with yourself too. If there is no way that your client can achieve what he or she wants (as assessed using your knowledge of the law and the courts) it is right that you should say so as soon as you have enough information to make a correct judgment. The interview must not drag on in the client's vague hope that all will be well if it is pushed hard enough. You may need to state that the result will be different from the expectation of the client but that you will, of course, do your level best to achieve the optimum outcome. You might say that what could be achieved is this rather than that, therefore you will tackle it in an appropriate way. The client may accept this as second best or may seek a second opinion, as is the client's right. Never belittle the client's opinion. Attempt to modify it using your knowledge and experience.

(g)   Some of your interviews may take place in a police cell (probably at 3 in the morning!). This demands a different approach although the basic principles are the same. Your care of the client is in ensuring that all the correct procedures are observed to the letter, as well as checking that allegations, from any source, are clearly and accurately identified. You are concerned with the client's interests and may be seen as the only friendly face in the place, as a safety net or as the route out of the cell, even if this is unlikely. Establish trust rapidly and ensure your credibility with the police and the client.

Your linguistic abilities will be tested as you interpret often garbled or streetwise accounts of events into legal terms. You will probably need an understanding of low English and current slang. Your approach can be very down-to-earth and realistic in order to reassure the client that you understand the situation. Your advice must be absolutely accurate as must your actions. Time-scales are very tight and much has to be accomplished in a shorter space of time than most matters allow. Never allow yourself to say, 'Of course you won't go down, you'll see'. Be honest and admit the likelihood of a custodial sentence, but promise to do whatever possible to reduce it.

5.29   JARGON AND LEGAL PROCEDURES

When asked why he got wet, the dinghy sailor said that he 'jibed all standing and ended in stays'. Perfectly good English words as such, but to a non-sailor, virtually incomprehensible. (He could have said that he fell into the sea when the sail clouted him as he was changing direction!) Every group, society, profession, sport and pastime has its own peculiar language designed to create an exclusivity amongst the aficionados whilst confusing or even excluding outsiders. A clear illustration of the confusions that can occur is in the use of the word 'induction' for instance. Ask an electrical engineer, a logician, a midwife and a training officer what the word means and you will have four completely different meanings, all of which derive from the Latin '*inducere*', to lead in.

Law is no exception to this habit of creating a unique vocabulary. The major difficulty for clients is that many of the words are ordinary English words which have special, exclusive meanings in legal conversation, such as 'pleading', 'action', 'party', 'distress', 'cognisance', 'opinion' and 'matter'. The last four have been used in this book in their broad English sense, rather than as legal terms.

There is no danger at all in using legal jargon amongst lawyers. Indeed the meanings of things are often clarified and refined by the use of jargon. Clients are rarely privy to this inner language and you should avoid using it without explanation. Be particularly careful with Latin phrases and exclusively legal words. When a particular legal word has to be used, in court for instance, then lead the client to it by describing the situation or effect and then explaining what it is known as in legal language. Having the word suddenly presented can cause confusion and lack of understanding.

If your clients do use legal words and phrases, check that they have the meaning correctly established in their minds. Some people in awe of lawyers will try to keep up and will use words they have heard without being totally *au fait* with the sense.

To an extent the same applies to legal procedures. Whilst these are extremely well-known to lawyers and many support staff, they are completely unknown quantities to the clients. They need to be explained carefully, in terminology that will not alarm or obfuscate. Never lose sight of the fact that you and your firm represent a lifeline to clients who are unable to unravel the convolutions and intricacies of law for themselves. They need your help and guidance and it is in their and your best interests to make the processes as understandable as possible. Explain the different functions of people involved in the case, the types of document used, the processes and interactions that take place.

5.30 KEEPING UP TO DATE WITH THE LAW

One of the most important elements of offering a sound legal service to your clients is to keep yourself right up to date with your chosen specialist areas of the law. Your training partner will be able to advise you on appropriate courses and other resources for maintaining your currency. Many organisations and institutions offer updating seminars and courses, maybe as part of your points-gathering programme. The 'trade press' is a rich source of information about procedural and legislated changes. As pointed out in chapter 6, you cannot afford to get it wrong.

5.31   LEGAL AID

A legally aided client will need to have the scheme explained. This can usefully be done by having a descriptive pamphlet available with the essential details clearly outlined (see also 5.38 on pamphlets). A major concern amongst clients with little or no money is how they can have access to a lawyer, particularly if there is no law centre near their home or workplace. Such clients coming to you will need reassurance that the system can help, within certain income limits.

Explain how the costs are worked out and how you charge your time. Tell the client also about the effect of the statutory charge and any possible contribution that may be required. Explain that if they lose the case, it is still possible for the court to order a contribution to their opponent's costs even if they are legally aided, and that if they win, their opponent may even so not pay all the costs. Warn legally aided clients of the consequences of not paying the required contribution.

5.32   LETTERS

A great deal of the law firm's work is conducted by (one might almost say 'driven by'!) letters and written material of all sorts. Much of it will be going to other lawyers in which case the language and style can be of a highly legal nature, as the recipients will have no trouble in understanding it. However, there will be many letters and memoranda going to clients or being copied for clients' approval and there, often, lies a problem. It is very hard to define exactly what good writing is – it may seem to be presumptuous for an author to even try a definition! However, there are rules for good writing although one person's view of a good letter or a fine and accurate piece of writing may not coincide with the views of another:

(a)   Precision – every word you place in a letter or draft must be there because it has a function. This may mean several rewrites, but the need to be accurate is of paramount importance.

(b)   Clarity – your letter should need to be read only once. The meaning should be clear from the first. Clarity of writing demands previous clarity of thought. The letter should be structured in a logical sequence of concepts or points so that the client can follow the thread without difficulty.

(c)   Language – the words used should be appropriate for the type of communication and not overladen with jargon or technical phrases. The language should be socially correct – a number of words and phrases are nowadays said to be provocative or discriminatory. The idea of 'political correctness' has received some caustic press, but the concepts are being adopted by more and more organisations wishing to rid their literature of possible bias, prejudice and unwanted 'isms'.

If you have difficulty in deciding the right word, then a book such as *Longman's Guide to English Usage* by Sidney Greenbaum and Janet Whitcut will offer sound advice and guidance.

(d)   Grammar – the rules of grammar are quite clear and should not be broken. If a client has to reread a piece because the structure of the sentences is wrong or clumsy then the fault is yours.

(e)   Punctuation – bad punctuation can ruin the meaning of a simple sentence. The most common errors are in the misuse of commas and semicolons, neither of which seem to be fully understood by many people.

(f)   Style – a good letter should be pleasing to look at as well as easy to read. It should be elegant. The layout should conform to current styles and should sit sensibly on the page. The current conventions of having all starting words left-justified and addresses presented without punctuation lead to a neatness of style and presentation. These conventions are also time-saving for typists (they probably invented them!).

You should have your reader in mind when writing. This will ensure that you choose a way of communicating that he or she will understand, just as you would if talking to them face to face.

(g)   Checking – never send a letter out without checking it carefully for errors. Even the best typist can make mistakes. Do not place too much reliance on your computer's spell-check. Many words have escaped the net because they were correctly spelled, but the wrong word in the circumstances.

A letter to an important client that ended 'I hope to see you again son' was passed as correct by the computer, but the recipient was not too pleased. Only later the writer discovered the missing 'o' in the last word!

5.33 LISTENING

One of the greatest services you can render to your clients, whether as receptionist, secretary or legal adviser is to listen creatively and constructively. Active listening is a subtle skill, but one which many people have not yet fully grasped.

The real skill comes in using your 'third ear' – the one which is the interpretive ear rather than the two crinkly protrusions on either side of your head. They merely act as funnels for the sound waves. Listen for the meaning and sense of what is being said and the feelings behind it, not merely the words used to convey the message. This involves concentration, attention, observation and participation. The interpretation of what is being said is aided if you can remove physical barriers to listening such as disturbances from elsewhere, your own tiredness or stress, a natural reluctance to listen to a boring or slow speaker and the adoption of non-conducive body language and posture.

Your client will expect you to ask questions but will also expect to be allowed to answer. Show your attention to the client by the correct, encouraging facial expressions and body posture. Nothing is worse when one is trying to make a point that is of great personal significance than the other person showing unmistakable signs of ennui, indifference and lost contact. Show your attentiveness by asking reflective questions and being alert and *interested*.

5.34 MESSAGES

In order to offer good service to your clients, you must include as a part of your normal routines and disciplines the accurate passing of messages. This sensible habit is equally important for receptionists and secretarial staff. Never take a message that is unclear to you – always ask for details to be repeated if they are indistinct or confusing. Always ask for the name of the originator and note any contact numbers or addresses. Ensure that the message is unambiguous and that it will be meaningful to the intended recipient. If there is a deadline for responding to a message, make sure that this is noted too.

The use of printed pro-forma message pads is recommended. Details can be entered against set headings, which in turn act as an agenda for taking the message. Dates and times of messages should be noted and the receiver should be identified in case any information needs to be checked.

Messages should be sent promptly and left where they will be readily seen. Message pads tend to be small so individual sheets are easily lost on a crowded desk. Fluorescent pads are very noticeable. Leave vital messages on yellow adhesive slips at eye level on office doors or on chair backs or outdoor coats.

One inventive firm introduced a range of four different coloured pads to indicate degrees of urgency for internal messages and memos, with pink as the most urgent. It was not long before more pink messages were being sent than all the others combined! One partner introduced a red spot sticker on his pink'uns to indicate 'extra urgent', until others started the same ploy. Eventually the whole idea was scrapped and all reverted to plain white pads. A case of overkill?

5.35 NEW BUSINESS

There are a number of activities and actions you can follow to help with the important matter of attracting new business. This can be new clients or more business from existing clients.

(a)   New clients should be welcomed – it is good news for the firm. Always check whether the client has been to you before in case there should be a conflict of interests.

You should always check whether a conflict arises in respect of new instructions, whether from a new client or one for whom you have acted in the past. For instance, it may be that this client wishes to sue an existing client of the firm. This check for possible conflict should be done before accepting instructions or when there are substantial changes in the nature of the job being handled, for example when an additional party is added to the transaction.

(b) Always treat any new enquiry as a matter of priority and remember that first impressions count a great deal. Hence the need for enthusiasm, courtesy and a willingness to help.

(c) Enquiries by letter must always be followed up expressing an interest in acting for the client. Telephone enquiries should be followed up swiftly – call back as soon as possible if you were not immediately available.

(d) Encourage any co-professional you deal with to recommend your firm, but ensure that the service you give justifies the recommendation. Reciprocate where possible. Clients deserve to be told about the best services of which you know. Always acknowledge introductions.

(e) Be alert for opportunities to gain new clients. Speak well of the firm when in company and emphasise its quality approach.

(f) With existing clients, describe other services that you or the firm offers that might be of interest. This shows a caring, proactive approach. Try to dissuade your clients from patronising other firms in the mistaken belief that you do not cover all their requirements.

5.36 NEW CLIENTS

The early stages of your relationship with new clients needs care and attention to detail. Remember that it often takes courage to visit a lawyer – the client may not be at his or her emotional or social best! Useful techniques for dealing with new clients include:

(a)   Never leave new clients waiting around. See them as soon as possible especially if you have a set appointment time. Existing clients may (just!) be more tolerant.

Reception staff have considerable responsibility for calming and reassuring the client in the first few minutes after arrival. Smile! Be welcoming and encouraging.

(b)   Set the client at ease with a moment or two of social chat and thank the client for choosing your firm. This will make him or her feel valued.

(c)   Be empathic – this means seeing life through their eyes and standing in their shoes without wishing to stay there. The client's point of view may be rather obscure to you but make every effort to understand it.

(d)   Be very thorough in your fact gathering. As yet, the client may not know the ropes and your guidance in the early stages is crucial to building rapport and trust and in setting standards for the relationship.

(e)   Remember the requirements under both rule 15 and the Written Professional Standards to inform your new client of the complaints procedures and the system for costing. (See 5.5 on billing and costs and chapter 6.)

The above points, whilst relevant to a client who is new to the firm, can also be applied to existing clients, whether they are giving new instructions or coming to a subsequent meeting.

5.37   NOTE TAKING

You will certainly have to take notes during your meetings with clients. Virtually no one has the ability to remember accurately entire conversations. Explain to your client that you will be making notes and that you will need a record of the meeting as an *aide-mémoire* when preparing the next stages. If carefully explained, this will be seen as a sensible and caring approach, in the client's best interests.

Do not let the note taking become the predominant part of the meeting as you will lose contact with the client and fail to recognise important signs, with your head down to the paper all the time. Write openly, not so that the client can read what you are writing but so that you can be seen writing. Furtive note taking can cause irritation and resentment.

In *Opinion Writing and Drafting*, one of Blackstone's books in the Inns of Court School of Law series, six important features of good notes are listed. They are included here with comments that are relevant to your client care practice:

(a)   Reasonable legibility – you will have to refer back to the notes and it is extremely irritating to find unintelligible squiggles where there should be words. Try to write better and faster. You do not want to go back to your client to ask again what you noted at the time but now cannot interpret.

(b)   Good organisation – random notes will not do. Organise the notes in groups of linked ideas. This will help later analysis.

(c)   Clear layout – use subheadings, underlinings, symbols, indented lists.

(d)   Comprehensive coverage – include all important points even if by just using key words. It is better to have all the points down in essence than to miss vital points whilst trying to write notes verbatim.

(e)   Selectivity – do not try to write down everything. Note all important points. Where exact wording is relevant, that must be noted.

(f)   Abbreviation – fast noting demands some form of understandable abbreviation, shorthand or speedwriting.

Try to develop a style of note taking that allows you to keep in good contact with the client whilst still writing. This might entail practice in having the paper and the client in broadly the same line of sight so that only your eyes need move. Try not to start writing notes right at the beginning of the session – allow the client to become established in the conversation first.

Always give yourself time at the end of an interview (before your next client enters breezily and blows away all your memory of the meeting!) to write up any important notes. This will involve some careful timing of your day, but will pay off in the end. It is difficult to write up notes of several meetings at one time, especially if they have been on broadly similar subjects. Confusion is very likely.

Several methods of note making can be recommended as part of the quality service to clients:

(a)   When the interview is about a matter which is familiar to you in that similar meetings take place regularly, or where the transaction can be expected to follow standard lines, prepare a *checklist* of questions to ask or topics to cover. This will help as an agenda for the meeting and will serve as a framework for note taking. Your clients will be impressed by your forethought and efficiency.

When taking instructions, a checklist of essential facts is useful to guarantee that the principal details are noted.

(b)   The *two-column method* is popular, where important points can be noted on the left side of the page with supporting notes on the right. A variation is to use three columns, key points, supporting points in favour and supporting points against.

(c)   A technique that is rapidly gaining favour in many walks of life is *mind-mapping*, originally proposed by Tony Buzan (see his book, *Use Your Head*, revised ed. (London: BBC/Ariel, 1988)). The essence of the method, illustrated in figure 5.6, is that the prime topic should be written in a central position on a page and the subtopics on stalks around it with associated ideas and comments being added in an ever widening pattern around the centre. The great advantages of this method coincide with the principles listed above – organisation and layout are clear, coverage can be complete and the whole exercise can be done with key words and linked themes. It also has the

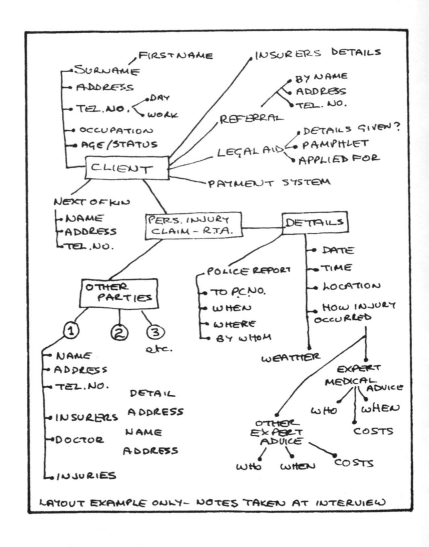

Figure 5.6   An example of notes made by mind-mapping

advantage of covering a complete topic (or conversation, lecture, speech preparation or research exercise) on one page. If a subtopic seems to be consuming a great deal of space, then it can be resited centrally on a fresh sheet and can be a mind-map in its own right. It is necessary to use neat and small handwriting but this is the only constraint.

5.38 PAMPHLETS

There are many occasions when a simply composed and attractively presented pamphlet could replace long verbal explanations about aspects of your service. They can also usefully be used as *aide-mémoires* to clients as they leave you, explaining procedures or actions that may ensue.

The range of topics is wide but could include areas such as:

— Information about the firm.
— Information about a particular department.
— The role of the solicitor.
— Services offered in languages other than English.
— Who will be dealing with your situation.
— Complaints procedures and the work of the SCB.
— The fee structure and methods of payment.
— Obtaining services under legal aid.
— The basic stages of conveyancing.
— Dealing with probate.
— Recent trends in environmental law.
— Coping with nuisance from your neighbours.

Once written in clear and unequivocal (and non-legal) language, these pamphlets can be printed with your firm's livery and logo and will form a vital part of the client care package. Pamphlets may be left at reception for the public to take at will, or for issue on a selective basis. You can also have a stock of pamphlets on your particular areas for use in explaining processes to your clients during an interview. The visual and explanatory nature of the brochure will serve as a useful aid, encouraging understanding and giving also a set of notes to take away.

5.39   PARKING

This is a contentious topic, especially in inner-city areas where parking is at a premium. Clients may be deterred from calling on you if they know that parking will be a major problem. If you are lucky enough to have a parking area for visitors, then it should be kept free for that purpose.

A London firm has an underground car park which it shares with another business in the same building. Clients who ask if there is convenient parking nearby have to be asked what sort of car they have, as the entrance to their part of the park is tortuous and cannot accommodate any car longer than 2.5 metres. That certainly sorts out the Bentley drivers from the Clios and Metros! As the nearest public car park is a good five minutes' walk away, some good custom may be lost if drivers are impatient about their time and tolerance of London parking. Sadly, this is a tale without a happy ending.

5.40   PRIVACY

Many clients who call on lawyers wish to do so in private. This takes two directions:

(a)   There should be no need for clients waiting to be seen by lawyers to be sat in a goldfish bowl of a reception area. Many firms have their reception at street level with large, clear windows. This may show to passers-by what fine taste in decor they have but it does not provide the seclusion from prying eyes that many clients crave. A waiting-room away from view is ideal, or better still, a number of small, comfortable rooms that can double when necessary as interview rooms. The prying eyes so feared by some people also belong to other clients!

(See also 5.45 on waiting-rooms.)

(b)   The interview itself should be conducted in private. If your firm does not provide exclusive offices, then interview rooms must be available. Clients generally do not wish to discuss their personal affairs within an environment that resembles the precinct room in *Hill*

Street Blues! Privacy does not only mean without other ears or eyes being able to encroach, it means without interruption. It is the least you can do for your clients.

5.41 QUESTIONING TECHNIQUES

Your purpose is to provide the best service possible to your client. Therefore you need to be able to find out in exact detail what is the nature of the problem and what are the major issues and complications. This demands a wide range of questioning techniques and skills.

Gathering information is a skilful process and you need to bear in mind that your client probably does not know precisely what information will be needed or in what depth you will need to probe. You are the guide through the exercise and you need to vary your style and tone of questioning as you progress. You may need to justify a question, if the client does not see its relevance.

Three broad styles of questioning are available: directive, patterned and non-directive – the choice of style depends on the situation and the desired outcome:

(a)   Directive questioning takes less time. It is appropriate for purely factual exchanges where the interviewer wants, and the client is willing to give. The client may possibly be on the defensive due to a lack of freedom with direct questions. This can impair the relationship as it tends to highlight differences.

(b)   Planned questioning leads to a planned conversation. It helps direct the interview along defined paths and is good for exchanging views.

(c)   Non-directive questioning takes more time. It explores sensitive matters, feelings and attitudes. It is used a great deal in counselling and is a far less formal approach.

Table 5.1 shows how these three styles of questioning may lead to differing patterns of interview and the range of possible reactions in your client.

	Directive	*Patterned*	*Non-directive*
Interviewer's role	Interrogator fact finder	Conversation guide	Counsellor listener
Relations with client	Boss – subordinate type	Equals working together	Helper
Latitude given to client to influence the interview	Very little control – more like acceptance	Some control as conversation changes directions	A great deal, as client can choose where to go next
Plan/agenda	Rigid adherence	Flexible within limits	Free, as either chooses
Sharing the talking	Interviewer sets the pace and directs the client	Interviewer supports and steers the client's flow	Interviewer supports flow, builds upon replies and waits out pauses
Types of question	High percentage of closed and leading questions	High percentage of open-ended, with some reflecting back questions	High percentage of reflecting back, with some open-ended questions
Net effect on client	Pressure, intimidation or closing-up	Sense of balance and give and take	Complete freedom and openness

Table 5.1   Styles of questioning

As an illustration of these different styles of questioning and their interrelatedness, figure 5.7 identifies examples on a continuum from directive to non-directive.

DIRECTIVE

Closed questions
Questions which produce
only short answers of
fact, like yes or no.

Examples
Did you see your
neighbour kick the
cat?

Leading questions
Questions which lead
the client to give the
answer that the lawyer
wants to hear.

I don't like cruelty
to animals – I don't
suppose you do either?

Controlling questions
Questions that guide
the conversation along
routes of the lawyer's
choosing.

Thank you for telling
me about the cat. Now
please tell me about
your neighbour and the
oak trees.

*Probing or building
questions*
Questions that build
upon an answer already
given, extending the
enquiry into a particular
subject.

Why did you say that
you liked people who
were kind to animals?

Open-ended questions
Questions which give
opportunity for a
lengthy answer.

What do you expect
the other people in
the village will say?

Reflecting-back questions
Questions which restate
a reply, to reopen the
topic or to check the
lawyer's understanding

So if the village folk
do run this petition,
you think it will
really help?

P
A
T
T
E
R
N
E
D

NON-DIRECTIVE

Figure 5.7   Styles of questioning

rolling questions' downwards, all the questions start with either 'Tell me about . . .' or with 'What', 'Why', 'Who', 'When' or 'Where'. You will find all the types of question very useful at different times during the conversation, leading your client through a maze of ideas and interests while arriving nearer and nearer to the complete spread of required information. Sometimes you will have to take a strong line and ask direct probing questions, especially if you feel that your client is covering something or being reticent.

5.42 RECEPTION SKILLS

We have said previously that receptionists are generally the first representatives of the firm to meet clients, whether they are new-comers or established visitors. This initial contact is vital in creating a sound relationship with the client.

This section is addressed directly to receptionists and others who act as the first contact point between the client and the firm. There are several important factors to consider in setting standards for reception skill and performance:

(a) Personal appearance must be in keeping with the general image that the firm wishes to promote whilst being comfortable to the individual and appropriate for the ambient temperature of the reception area. Rules about what to wear are impossibly difficult, but most receptionists will recognise that they have a major role in being first in line in the chain of contact for the client. This demands style and propriety within current business fashion trends. Words such as neat, well-groomed and smart come to mind, but they are very imprecise. Whether a man or a woman, the receptionist must not deter people from coming in!

(b) Personal style is important. A recent survey of experienced receptionists resulted in the following list of desirable characteristics:

reliable	informative	friendly
helpful	accommodating (!)	efficient
experienced	modern	client oriented
dynamic	patient	polite

caring	tactful	confident
competent	knowledgeable	adroit
unflappable	cheerful	adaptable
multi-talented	indispensable (!)	tidy

Most of these are indeed necessary characteristics, indicating the varied nature of reception work. A client entering the firm's premises for the first time must be encouraged to stay. The way the receptionist operates will play a large part in the client's decision.

(c) The tidiness and apparent efficiency of the reception service will influence the client.

(d) Greetings are important. A smile is absolutely necessary. Clients will be pleased to offer their names, and will then expect to be addressed correctly. Regular clients will expect to be greeted by name after a few visits.

(e) No client should have to hover about the reception area while the receptionist attends to other matters. Promptness is important.

(f) Once the client is welcomed and contact has been made with the appropriate adviser, the client should be told whether to wait and for how long, or directed or escorted to the meeting. If the waiting becomes prolonged, it is the receptionist who usually has to take the brunt of the client's distress. Tact and concern are needed, with every effort being made, and being seen to be made, to hasten the meeting.

(g) New clients often come in very agitated or anxious about seeing a lawyer. They may ask what the solicitor is like, as if he or she was expected to have two heads or the ability to breathe fire! (Some can!) Many people put visiting the solicitor in the same vein as going to the dentist with the same levels of apprehension and angst. It is the receptionist who has to deal with these feelings in the first instance. The way they are dealt with will undoubtedly help or hinder the eventual relationship, according to the success or otherwise of this first encounter.

(h) Some firms have considered issuing corporate uniforms to reception staff, but this has not generally been well received as an idea by the receptionists themselves. It has been very successfully applied in many service industries, such as building societies and banks. The arguments usually range from 'excessively regimented' to 'creates a professional and smart image'.

(i)   General duties of the receptionist may include:

(i)   welcoming and looking after visitors,

(ii)   maintaining the visitors' book,

(iii)   operating a switchboard,

(iv)   issuing literature to callers,

(v)   dealing with mail,

(vi)   receiving front-door deliveries,

(vii)   watching out for lapses in security or safety,

(viii) being alert for accidents, threats or unwanted intrusion,

(ix)   shielding lawyers and staff from unwelcome visitors, time-wasters and cranks (these latter have a cunning habit of entering warm, dry buildings to while away time with no regard for the workers within, especially on cold, wet days),

(x)   receiving and passing on messages,

(xi)   maintaining the reception area in a tidy and safe condition.

(j)   It is a tragic reflection of today's society that receptionists should be advised about dealing with bomb threats or deliberate attack or assault. However, telephone messages do sometimes arrive which could be very threatening. People can choose to live by violence. Remember that you will have clients on the premises as well as members of the firm.

If you receive a bomb threat:

(i)   As a matter of urgency, attract the attention of someone in authority who can in turn contact the emergency services and BT.

(ii)   Try to keep the person talking for as long as you can.

(iii)   Listen intently for clues about the caller:

— Gender, age, nationality, accent?
— Manner and tone – nervous, frightened, drunk, confident, cocky?
— Background noises or clues about location?
— Ad-libbing or reading from a script?

(iv)   Listen carefully to the message – you may need to recall it verbatim later on.

(v)   Try to elicit name, address, location of bomb, timing, appearance, reason for the threat and why us? Ask how you can know the threat is true.

(k)   The following 'rules' for receptionists have been found to be a useful guide:

1   Smile.
2   Never stop learning the receptionist's job.
3   Always stay cool and calm, even in the face of bluster and unreasonableness.
4   Address clients by name wherever possible and get their titles right.
5   Take good care of clients on the way in and the way out.
6   Always give a good impression of yourself and the firm.
7   Be an absolute mine of information about the firm.
8   Be ever vigilant for lapses in security or safety.
9   Never leave the reception area unattended.
10   Always write down messages and deliver them on time.
11   Remember that you are on display in the firm's shop window.
12   Keep smiling!

5.43 TELEPHONE STYLE

Telephoning presents more problems in its way than face-to-face
conversation. The immediate difference is the loss of visual contact,
and until videophones become common, the task of establishing
rapport and mutual dependence is more difficult. When you consider
how much ordinary conversation depends on facial and bodily signs
for meanings, feelings and reactions, the determination of these from
mere heard words is a complex task. In spite of BT's insistence that
its system is the best in the world, lines are still foggy and crackles
and blips do occur.

There are several techniques that can be used to enhance an otherwise
imperfect communications medium and give good service to your
clients. First some ideas for the initial speaker, whether this is the
telephonist or you:

(a)   With incoming calls, make sure that you are fully connected
before speaking, lest your opening words are lost in the crackle of
connecting.

*The telephonists in one firm with a large switchboard have not
grasped the necessity to do this. Consequently callers usually hear
'%$½?@kksc@%?..n I help you?' The callers then have to ask
whether they are connected to the firm they thought they were calling
to start the conversation again. This is irritating and time-wasting.*

(b)   Have a standard greeting for the telephone. Current fashion
seems to be to have a four part greeting: 'Good morning/afternoon
... Grabbit Fleecem Solicitors ... My name is Julie ... How can I help
you?' This is often said in a singsong voice with absolutely no feeling
whatever. It is not pleasant to hear. Certainly the name of the firm
needs to be mentioned to establish the correct connection. A greeting
should be included. The name of the telephonist is not needed.

An ideal response is therefore 'Good morning/afternoon. Grabbit
Fleecem Solicitors. Can I help you?' The greeting allows the voice to
be heard and is dispensable if the phone lines are not too good and
gives time for things to settle down before the firm's name is given.
The last enquiry is optional, but friendly.

(c)   The greeting and name announcement *must* be said with a smile and with feeling. You really *do* want to speak to the caller! Smiling does transmit over the phone lines and creates a welcoming opening to what may be a difficult conversation.

(d)   Always stay in conversation with the caller until you have made the necessary connections, even if it is punctuated with absences to deal with other calls. This is much preferable to electronic Bach with no indication of how long it may continue. (Brandenburg 3 is great but not played one note at a time on a toy keyboard!) Never leave the caller hanging on without knowing what is happening. Even if it proves difficult to make the connection the client seeks, keep smiling.

(e)   Never cover the mouthpiece to curse about people not being where they should be when wanted. Very few hands are soundproof.

(f)   Always be polite to callers even if they become abusive or hostile. Unfortunately you are the firm in the eyes of the caller so you will receive all the flak. Do not lose your cool; try to respond calmly. Never lay blame off elsewhere – explain in businesslike terms that it is difficult to make the connection but that you will try again and keep the caller informed. Always tell the eventual receiver of the call that the caller has had trouble (and was rude or belligerent if that was the case). Remember that a rancorous start to a call can sour the whole transaction.

(g)   When your switchboard is very busy, it is effective to have a call sequencer in operation. Callers are linked to the firm and informed by a recorded message that there will be a slight delay but that they will be dealt with in turn. No caller is lost because of tedious hanging on.

There are techniques that help with telephone calls once the caller is through to the lawyer:

(h)   Use a clearer voice than for face-to-face conversation, with changes in tone and pitch. Always sound alert and confident – this will encourage the client to follow suit.

(i)   Listen intently. You only have shifts in the client's tone and pace to assist you to judge his or her mood, attitude or veracity.

(j)   Use the same questioning styles discussed in 5.41 and check frequently that you are receiving the correct messages.

(k)   A psychologically sound and personally encouraging technique is to stand whilst speaking on the telephone. The improved posture helps with voice control and imparts an authoritative air. Similarly, it is posited that being correctly dressed helps with telephone interviewing. Being correctly attired means that you will feel confident and will speak accordingly. Many telesales companies insist that their telephone users dress formally for the telephone, reminiscent of Lord Reith and his insistence on BBC announcers wearing DJs. He had a point.

(l)   When initiating calls, always prepare yourself well with an agenda, accurate notes and a set of questions to be asked. This helps also with note taking. If the call is likely to be complicated, with a need for the client to refer to materials at that end, it is courteous and caring to call ahead and suggest that certain papers be gathered ready for you when you telephone back in a short while.

5.44   THIRD PARTIES

Your communications with third parties have a direct bearing on the way your clients judge your work for them. You must be absolutely certain that your activities are entirely correct, especially if fees or disbursements are concerned.

(a)   If you are instructing a third party on behalf of your client and you are expecting your client to pay, be sure you have the appropriate instructions first.

(b)   Always make it quite clear who will be paying when you send the instruction.

(c)   Be sure to mention any appropriate time-limits. (See also chapter 6.)

(d)   Never stoop to acrimonious correspondence. Even if you feel better for it, it is unlikely to further your client's cause and you will have to put in a bill for something that cannot really be called a service.

(e)   On the client's behalf, always pay third-party accounts promptly. If this is not going to be possible explain why at the outset. Generally, third-party accounts should not be paid unless funds are received from your client, so anticipate this and have funds in readiness.

5.45   WAITING ROOMS

The term 'waiting-room' tends to conjure up an image of a gloomy, sooty, spare and unwelcoming room on Crewe station in the days of steam. Sadly, many 1990s solicitors' waiting-rooms are little better. Clients need to be given somewhere comfortable and warm to wait, especially if the waiting is likely to be prolonged.

Many firms have risen to this requirement and have provided a room or rooms for visitors that are pleasant and well-equipped. Some rooms can usefully double as interview rooms. Drinks dispensers are often welcome. Something to read should be available, but material that is appropriate to the client groups. Furtive Fred the burglar will not be impressed by *Country Life* (unless it gives him ideas for the next job!), and Sir Thomas will not wish to be stuck with *Whippets Monthly*. Magazines for all anticipated tastes is the rule, but nothing more than three months out of date, with something for children also. This may seem like another expense to be added to overheads but most firm's partners and staff receive between them dozens of publications on a regular basis. A simple survey could discover many sources of appropriate reading matter at little cost and effort.

A number of firms have introduced piped music into their waiting-rooms and reception areas. Given the right type of music played at the correct volume, the psychological effect of the calming back-ground noise has proved to be effective. With the emotive messages in many songs, both pop and classical, the choice needs to be made carefully. There are many professionally produced tapes or CDs that are designed for such purposes and the effects of music on the buying/waiting/lift-travelling/dentist-visiting public are well researched and documented.

5.46   WHO DOES WHAT?

Clients are often not clear about who does what in a solicitor's office.

A pamphlet could be produced which clearly explains the different roles to be found in your practice (see 5.38).

An essential part of the relationship between client and lawyer is to clarify the areas of responsibility and inform the client carefully which colleagues will be doing which bits and why. You must make a point of informing your clients if any changes in personnel on the case occur and explain why this has been necessary. If possible, effect an introduction to relevant colleagues when the client calls.

Chapter Six

Dealing with Complaints

6.1 ABOUT BALLOONS

In *Customer Care Management* by Andrew Brown, the writer likens a client to a balloon, which is easily handled in its uninflated state. When it is full of air or puffed up with anger or disappointment, it cannot be put into your pocket any more. You have three choices of action:

(a)   An immediate answer would be to burst it, just for the hell of it. The instant result is no balloon – and no client either!

(b)   You could just let it go in which case it will splutter about all over the place until all the puff has gone out of it. As an uncontrolled flying object it could end up anywhere, with the senior partner, the Law Society, blasting off at clients waiting patiently in reception (heaven forbid!) or carping on about your inadequacies on a television consumer programme.

(c)   The best option is to hang on to your balloon and let the air out slowly and under control until you can put the balloon back in your pocket.

This chapter is principally about option (c).

6.2 RULE 15 (CLIENT CARE)

Practice Rule 15 states:

(1)   Every principal in private practice shall operate a complaints handling procedure which shall, *inter alia*, ensure that clients are informed whom to approach in the event of any problem with the service provided.

(2)   Every solicitor in private practice shall, unless it is inappropriate in the circumstances:

(a)   ensure that clients know the name and status of the person responsible for the day-to-day conduct of the matter and the principal responsible for its overall supervision;

(b)   ensure that clients know whom to approach in the event of any problem with the service provided;

(c)   ensure that clients are at all relevant times given any appropriate information as to the issues raised and the progress of the matter.

Several aspects of this rule have been covered in the text, but in summary:

(a)   Tell your client at the outset of the matter what the procedures are for complaint in case of problems. (This can be done with a pamphlet.)

(b)   Give to your client the name of the person to contact, preferably in writing.

(c)   Make sure that established clients know of the procedures.

(d)   It is not required to have your complaints procedures written down, but it is preferable. The major elements should be:

(i)   Clients should be advised to make known any problems.

(ii) Clients should know whom to approach with problems.

(iii) Complaints must be investigated thoroughly and promptly and the client informed of actions taken.

(iv) Clients should be told that they can take the complaint to the Solicitors Complaints Bureau if not satisfied.

6.3 DEALING WITH COMPLAINTS

Translating the slow deflation of the balloon in the light of Practice Rule 15 involves a range of activities and approaches:

(a) Show concern that the problem exists, but do not apologise or take any blame until you are certain that a problem actually exists.

(b) Permit the client to explain the gist of the problem without interruption, then seek elaboration of any facts that are unclear to you.

(c) Once the problem is clear, agree a course of action that the client feels is appropriate and that is within your firm's stated procedures for complaints.

(d) Take necessary actions, keep the client informed and, if the matter is resolved, make the required report and file appropriately. If further action is needed, promptly take the required steps and inform the principal supervising the matter.

(e) Never at any stage apportion blame to colleagues or 'the system' or the computer. If you are the right person for the client to complain to, then you have the problem until it is resolved.

(f) Dealing with complaints is a good test of your client care policies and may well be seen as such by complaining clients. Clients whose complaints were well-handled and resolved will probably stay with you, whereas dissatisfied complainers will certainly leave and may take others with them (vicarious bad publicity).

One firm has cause to thank its receptionist for an intuitive and creative approach to complaining clients. When she realises that the client is about to complain rather than make an ordinary call, she asks the caller to hang up so that she can call back, saying, 'You don't want to have to pay for a call like this, let us pay for it. I will call you back directly.' By the time she does so, often the client has calmed down and can talk more rationally whilst appreciating the firm's acceptance of the costs of the call. Clever!

6.4   COMPLAINT AVOIDANCE

A number of accident black spots exist in all firms – those procedures or operations where something is likely to go wrong. Many can be rectified by careful planning and better communications.

Activities to reduce black-spot events and other complaint-generating activities include:

(a) Communicate! The first annual report of the Solicitors Complaints Bureau stated that a major cause of complaints was a breakdown in communications between client and solicitor. It continued, 'About 90 per cent of complaints are resolved immediately, once the client understands what has been going on. Some of the complaints would never have been made if the solicitor had explained to the client what was happening, or if the client had asked.'

(b)   Better supervision and checking of incoming and outgoing mail.

(c)   Greater attention to detail when giving undertakings

(d)   Closer supervision of tasks delegated to junior fee-earners. and other staff.

(e)   Closer control of files passing between departments.

(f)   Greater attention to swift resolution of problems.

(g)   More care in keeping up to date with current law and procedures.

Dealing with Complaints

(h)   Greater care in identifying, specifying and notifying and others about time-limits (in both contentious and non-contious work).

(i)   More regular attention to 'problem' files.

(j)   Avoiding unnecessary delays.

(k)   Improving standards of personal and departmental office keeping and organisation.

(l)   Improved prioritising.

(m)   Improved message taking and delivery. Improved action upon the receipt of messages.

(n)   Doing all the other things that this book talks about and doing them with verve, conviction and commitment!

Chapter Seven

Evaluation

7.1 AREAS FOR EVALUATION

So, the new programme of improved client care has been installed and the training has taken place. It is necessary to find out what are the effects on the firm. The scheme was after all devised to increase the client database, improve the bottom line and secure the future.

Evaluation in the short term is almost impossible if it is to be done in financial terms. Most of the reviewing processes will define and explore feelings rather than facts. They are still valuable methods, though, and lack of hard data does not invalidate the inquiry.

7.1.1 Measurable effects

Careful analysis of several fields of data will reveal information that can place a worth on the client care programme:

(a) Income – the ultimate measure, but one for long-term analysis. An increase in fee receipts that occurs alongside a purposeful programme of increased client care could be merely coincidental. However, there is likely to be a correlation.

(b) Client base – the many factors that go towards a sound client care programme with its consequent greater public profile for the firm can encourage more clients to seek help.

(c)   Thank-you letters and positive comments about the services rendered – these can be listed and counted and compared with previous periods. A reduction in the number of complaints also provides a measure of the effectiveness of the campaign.

(d)   Referrals – personal referral is a powerful way for a business to expand. If properly encouraged to speak well of the firm after a matter is satisfactorily dealt with, a contented client is a useful ambassador. Referrals will increase accordingly.

(e)   Recommendations – major clients and co-professionals who have been well cared for will recommend your firm if they are also satisfied with what you do.

(f)   Enquiries – telephone staff should be encouraged to log enquiries before and after a major client care programme is started. Handled well, these should become clients and increases can be noted.

7.1.2   Non-measurable effects

Some results from an increased awareness of client care are not quantifiable mathematically:

(a)   Internal climate – one of the concomitant changes that a client care scheme ought to engender is an improvement in colleague care and a general warming of the climate within the firm. This can be revealed as a reduction of internal friction (between people, between sections or between departments), an increase in cooperation and mutual support and more smiling!

(b)   Increased job satisfaction – there is no doubt that improved client care makes for better feelings about the job. This greater satisfaction derives from the reduction in difficulties and prickliness when the lawyer-client relationship is smoother and more positive.

(c)   Behavioural changes – the emphasis on client care can bring about remarkable changes in people. You may notice changes in yourself and the way you approach and deal with clients. Other people may be demonstrating changed behaviour also, which makes for more pleasant working conditions.

One old campaigner seemed to be quite resistant to 'all this nonsense about client care' and very grudgingly took the firm's new client care handbook away after the seminars. Not long afterwards he was observed, when he thought he was not being observed, actually being really pleasant to one of his clients with whom he had had a running battle of wits for years. That in its turn cheered everyone else up and in time he changed permanently for the better, although he never admitted the source of his new-found approaches!

These internal changes can be reviewed by means of a questionnaire. This could be completed anonymously although it would be hoped that, with the improved relationships and greater openness that a care scheme should engender, no one should be afraid of making helpful if critical comments.

7.2   WHAT ARE THE CLIENTS' VIEWS?

Conducting client satisfaction surveys can be an emotive issue. Traditionalists may argue that it is not ethical to canvass views from clients about their opinions of the firm. In an ever more competitive world, it is important to know how well clients are being served, from their perception. Maybe adverse comments will be received anyway by the firm (usually about billing!) but brickbats are easier to throw than accolades. A real client opinion poll will reveal a wealth of ideas about issues of specific interest to the firm. Praise may be given; then successful strategies can be developed further. Complaints and grumbles can be painful but should precipitate corrective actions.

The simplest way of conducting a client survey is with a carefully constructed questionnaire. This can be sent to selected clients – but not only those where a favourable response can be expected! Avoid sending questionnaires to clients where the matter dealt with was particularly sensitive or distressing – there is no need to open old wounds. A generally well-received procedure is for a partner to complete the questionnaire in conversation with a client. The public relations aspects of this approach are very valuable and can help to cement relationships further although it is extravagant on time.

Many of the high-street banks now leave client opinion question-naires on the counter for completion by those who feel the urge to do so. This tends to have the effect of generating only comments that are critical of the bank. Very few people will bother to take a question-naire to complete if they have no problems about which to grouse. If you choose to leave some survey sheets at reception, it would certainly show that you took the canvassing of client opinion seriously.

7.2.1 Designing questionnaires

There are a number of principles around the compilation and use of client surveys:

(a) The questionnaire must be simple. The value is lost if it commands too much of the client's time. Questions should be limited to around a dozen. Using tick-boxes rather than asking for narrative answers speeds the operation but tends to limit the range of possible responses. If suggestions are made about possible replies to a given question, these should be listed randomly rather than in scalar form from worst scenario to best. This also precludes the respondent from ticking all the middle boxes in a bland, average, meaningless pattern. (See figure 7.1.)

(b) Where tick-boxes are used, there should also be a space for the respondent to make comments if so inclined.

(c) The questionnaire must be visually attractive, filling it in should be a pleasant task. It should have an appealing layout but still amply represent the firm's house style and the seriousness of the exercise. The questions need to be very carefully thought out and composed, after the purposes of the survey have been quite clearly identified.

(d) The return of the questionnaires must be facilitated by prepaid envelopes – the client cannot be expected to contribute anything but a little time to the exercise.

(e) It is difficult to offer the clients anything for taking part in the survey, other than a small token of appreciation. Many publicity companies now produce inexpensive company-personalised gifts such as printed desk calendars or pen containers. Research will reveal many small but dignified gifts ('freebies') that can be posted at little additional cost. Such hand-outs are a reminder to the client of the firm's existence and can usefully incorporate telephone and fax numbers and other relevant contact information. Thanks must certainly be given, whether accompanied by a gift or not, and, as a good piece of PR, this should be an extra communication after the response is received.

(f)   The letter accompanying the questionnaire must emphasise the confidential nature of the survey. It should point out that such information can greatly assist the firm to update and improve its services and care to clients, thereby benefiting clients and staff accordingly. The letter should be sent out over the senior partner's signature, preferably with each individually signed.

(g)   A secretariat should be set up to process the exercise and arrangements must be made for collating the information received.

The compilers of a client satisfaction questionnaire in a firm must choose questions that reflect the areas of inquiry being followed and which will provide data leading to action. An example of a questionnaire with suggested answers is shown in figure 7.1 (only the first few questions are shown in full).

Please tick any of the comments that describe your feelings or reactions, or make a comment if that would be fairer.

1   Why did you choose this firm in the first place?

local reputation ☐ recommended ☐ advertisement ☐
Yellow Pages ☐ saw the offices ☐ heard the name ☐
previously with (merged firm) ☐

other reason [＿＿＿＿＿＿＿＿＿＿＿＿＿＿＿＿＿＿＿＿＿]

2   How did you make the first contact with us?

by telephone ☐ by letter ☐ made an appointment ☐
called in the office ☐

other [＿＿＿＿＿＿＿＿＿＿＿＿＿＿＿＿＿＿＿＿＿＿＿]

3   On your first visit to our offices, how did you feel about:

(a)   the offices and building?

impressive ☐ cold and impersonal ☐ overwhelming ☐
welcoming ☐ mediocre ☐ too plush ☐ pleasant ☐

other feelings ☐_____☐

(b)   the reception that you received?

intimidating ☐ friendly ☐ calming ☐ efficient ☐
uninterested ☐ distant ☐

other feelings ☐_____☐

4   Was it made clear to you right at the beginning who you would
be dealing with?

rather confusing ☐ very clear ☐ too many names ☐
names and positions identified ☐ no names given ☐

other comments ☐_____☐

Figure 7.1   Start of a questionnaire for a client survey

Other questions can cover such matters as:

(a)   Did the partners and staff you met deal with your matter
efficiently and swiftly?

(b)   Once you had begun to know us better, did your opinions
change?

(c)   As your matter progressed, did we keep you informed of
developments and any changes in personnel on your case.

(d)   Were the fees reasonable and did you understand the bill?

(e)   How do we compare with other law firms with whom you have had contact?

(f)   How did we react to your particular situation or problem?

(g)   Were you satisfied overall with the way your matter was dealt with by this firm?

(h)   Would you recommend us to others?

(i)   Were there any differences between the way the partners and the secretarial and reception staff dealt with you?

(j)   Would you return to us in the future should the need for legal services arise?

The information gathered from both internal and external sources of research can be used by the firm creatively to review its policy on client care and as a solid base upon which to redesign or re-emphasise specific care practices.

Bibliography

Books referred to in the text

Buzan, Tony, *Use Your Head*, new ed. (London: Ariel/BBC, 1988).
Ellis, Jean, *Citizens Advice Bureaux Service to Black Clients* (London: NACAB, 1992).
Inns of Court School of Law, *Opinion Writing and Drafting*, 3rd ed. (London: Blackstone, 1991).
Law Society, *Equal Opportunities in Law Firms* (London: Law Society, 1989).
Law Society, *Quality: a Briefing for Solicitors* (London: Law Society, 1989).
Law Society, *The Race Report* (London: Law Society, 1989).
Pannett, Alan, *Managing a Law Firm* (Legal Practice Handbook) (London: Blackstone, 1992).
Peters, Tom, and Austin, Nancy, *A Passion for Excellence* (London: Fontana, 1989).
Rogers, Carl, *On Becoming a Person* (London: Constable, 1961).
Twist, Helena, *Effective Interviewing* (Legal Practice Handbook) (London: Blackstone, 1992).

Further reading

Other useful material can be found in the following books:

Garratt, Sally, *Manage Your Time* (London: Fontana, 1985).
Pease, Allan, *Body Language* (London: Sheldon Press, 1985).

Seddon, John, *I Want You to Cheat — The Unreasonable Guide to Service and Quality in Organisations* (Buckingham: Vanguard Press, 1992).
Sorrensen, Gregory, *Ten Keys to Dynamic Customer Relations* (London: Kogan Page, 1988).